I Once Met

Fifty Encounters with The Famous

Edited by Richard Ingrams

In Stuart
with love
from
Richard

Oct 96

Oldie Publications Ltd
London

This compilation first published by
Oldie Publications Ltd

Copyright © 1996 Oldie Publications Ltd

The publishers would like to thank the respective copyright owners
for permission to include articles in this volume

A CIP catalogue record for this book is available from
The British Library

ISBN 1 901170 02 0

Covers printed by Amica Fine Print Ltd
Text printed and bound by Woolnough Bookbinding Ltd
Design and production by Richard Adams Associates
Cover design by Stephen Shotton

Contents

Introduction

J AMES MICHIE (POET and publisher) had a brilliant idea during his, alas, brief spell as the *Oldie*'s literary editor. The title said it all. 'I Once Met' would describe a single meeting with a famous person which would reveal that famous person in an interesting/unusual light. James, when working as an editor at Bodley Head, had helped Charlie Chaplin to write his autobiography, and offered to kick the series off with his account of the famous clown. I think I commissioned one or two more.

But the feature had not been long in existence before the readers caught on and began to send in their own stories. Being an editor who has tried to react more positively to the 'unsolicited' than most of my confreres I was naturally delighted by this development. It transpired that, with one or two exceptions, the 'I Once Mets' submitted by those people normally described as 'ordinary' were much more interesting than those by the professional journalist or biographer.

One reason perhaps was that the famous person was off his guard and unaware that he was being observed. However as someone who has dabbled in biography I am well aware that the most revealing anecdotes will almost always come from the least expected quarter which is what makes writing biographies a frustrating business. I can imagine Lord Montgomery's biographer would have given anything to have had David Ransom's encounter (as a schoolboy) with the Field Marshal. Wouldn't Andrew Motion who wrote the life of Philip Larkin have loved to know how his hero stole and defaced Glyn Lloyd's priceless cigarette cards?

It remains for me to thank all those who have contributed to the series and to hope that this little book will inspire others to write in.

Richard Ingrams
July 1996

Louis Armstrong

by Bob Lord

HE FIRST APPEARED here at the Holborn Empire, some time around 1932, as I remember. Then he was known as a 'Jazz' player, so this handkerchief-waving, perspiring coloured star was a little too outré for the Palladium. He was featured down the road at Moss Empires No 2, as a soloist fronting a group of picked British swingers.

Their string bass player was Spike Hughes, also an A&R man, who led one of our first jazz groups recording on a major label, his 'Deccadents'. At the time I was pestering him to give me lessons and actually had a few, mostly with a cue on the snooker tables in the Six Bells, next to the recording studio. On this occasion, Spike asked me to help him.

He had a morning session to record the Ambrose band with Evelyn Dahl singing, and he feared possible difficulties and even rewriting of the musical arrangements to get them together. So he asked me to go to the theatre in case he was delayed, get his fiddle ready and stand by to deputise. Of course he made it, so we stood outside Louis' dressing room listening to the wonderful, unforgettable sound of him warming up, together with his band.

When that smiling, jovial face full of flashing teeth came out and joined us, Satchmo was carrying a cigarette twice as fat and as long as any Craven A, and he passed it round for us whiteys to try. He had been brought up on the stuff – one of his finest recordings was entitled 'Muggles', another name for pot.

But when one of his now happy backing group went for a second drag, that smiling face turned livid. Almost viciously he grabbed back the roach, shook it in the offender's face and spat out: 'Man, if you use dat shit, you use dat shit, you don't let dat shit use you!'

Jean Louis Barrault

by David A Read

N 1963 I was chief electrician at the Aldwych theatre, which was leased to the Royal Shakespeare Company, who played there from September to June. In the remaining summer months Peter Daubeny presented his World Theatre Season. Compared to the RSC season, this was a doddle. The same show every night for a week, and a ready-made one at that. We still had to work every weekend of course, but that was money in the bank, boozer or betting shop, depending on your inclinations.

The 'Theatre de France' arrived at about midnight on Saturday with a lot of Gallic flap and fluster. The set was erected, the lamps were hung, coloured and focused, and by Monday morning we were ready for the lighting session, which was to be conducted by the director, Monsieur Jean Louis Barrault.

Monsieur Barrault eventually appeared and we duly set to work. Things went well throughout the morning, so we took a short lunch break and then continued in the afternoon.

Theatre directors treat electricians, carpenters and the like in one of two ways. They either ignore you completely for the most part and then say 'I suppose the electricians are all in the pub' when you are standing beside them. Or, worse still, they treat you like some beloved family retainer who is slightly dotty and has to be cajoled into everything. Both types have an irritating mannerism. They say 'Can we?' when they mean 'Will you?' Some of the muttered responses I've heard to 'Can we sweep the stage?' would unnerve a brewer's drayman.

The famous Frenchman was very different. For one thing, he wouldn't stand still. One minute he'd be on stage checking something and the next his voice would come from the back of the upper circle telling us to throw some lamp out of focus because it was making ugly lines on the floor. He kept up a continuous dialogue with his stage management and various administrative people who wandered on and off stage throughout the day. He spoke to me and my crew either through Maggie or in a mixture of English and carefully pronounced French. He was a whirlwind of a man who seemed to have tons of time for everyone and everything.

Towards the end of the day things slowed down a lot and I expressed concern that we were running a bit late and that I'd have to break the crew before the performance.

He turned to the stage and shouted some rapid French. It had an immediate effect and the proceedings moved on apace. I asked Maggie what he had said.

She wasn't sure, so we enquired. 'Ah!' he said. 'It is a very useful expression. What is the word you use meaning to make love to a woman?' Maggie, who had been properly brought up, said, 'Oh dear! I suppose you mean "fuck".'

Exactly, he said. 'I told them to stop trying to fuck a fly. You must have a similar expression in English. No?'

Maggie thought for a bit and then said, 'I suppose our closest would be "to split hairs".' We all agreed that *'arretez d'enculer les mouches'* had much more style.

At about 4.30pm Barrault stopped and told me to give the crew a break. I said that as there was very little left to do we might as well finish it. 'No,' he said. 'Tell your men to go home and make babies. We can finish when they come back.' I obviously didn't look too happy about the idea because he gave me some advice. 'On a first night to have nervous actors is a good thing. To have nervous technicians is a disaster.'

I have never forgotten that remark and have had cause to repeat it once or twice when faced with bad directions from men of less talent and wisdom. We finished our work on time. The curtain rose and on came the indefatigable Jean Louis to give a splendid three-hour performance. I don't know if any babies were made.

Lord Beveridge
by C J Newson

I WAS SUMMONED one day to see Lord Beveridge to discuss a resumption of his *History of Prices and Wages,* which had been in abeyance for a decade or three (I was academic editor for Longman, which had published Volume One). I took the Oxford train, off which I was to be met. A Rolls? Rugs over the knees in the back? There was no chauffeur at the barrier, no clue! Suddenly I heard my name, and Lord B appeared, waving a stick. 'Come on, my boy. Jump in!' We got into a post-war saloon, of uncertain age, Lord B at the wheel. We shot out of the station and came to rest with the bonnet under the tail of a lorry stalled in Walton Street. Later he described an arc in the road outside his house, mounted the pavement, just missing the garden fence. and came to rest in an orderly fashion. The manoeuvre reminded him of some obscure episode with the Duke of Northumberland, which amused him greatly.

Once in his study, he seized a bottle of Spanish brandy, and waved vaguely at a mass of filing cabinets which filled half the room, as he poured some generous pre-prandial drinks. 'The Beveridge Report, my boy!' He then made an extremely ungenerous remark about its beneficiaries . . . 'Bloody workers! They expect something for nothing.'

Lunch was announced, and it was accompanied by a extremely good claret. He indicated a desire to lie down, and so withdrew. An hour or two was spent talking to his female companion and research assistant, after which we thought we ought 'just to check'. Lord Beveridge was lying on the floor, wrapped up in a plaid before the fire, asleep. 'You'd better go!' she said.

I caught the early evening train, and later thought I ought to ring up. 'I've called the doctor, and he's been taken to hospital.' He died not very much later. Never, in his indubitable high excitement on that day, did we talk about his *History of Prices and Wages*.

A lovely man! Thirty years later, I often pass his old Northumberland house on the way to Bamburgh, and think of him still.

Augustine Birrell
by Magdalen Goffin

I N HIS DAY Augustine Birrell was a celebrity. Raymond Mortimer once remarked that he looked like Thackeray but talked like Dr Johnson. As Chief Secretary for Ireland in Asquith's administration, he was a member of a brilliant cabinet which included Sir Edward Grey, John Morley, Lloyd George and the young Winston Churchill.

Ireland, however, that running sore in England's flesh, proved to be Birrell's political undoing. Estimates of his tenure of office vary, but either through indolence or reliance on the wrong advice, he failed to foresee the likelihood of the Easter Rising in 1916 and therefore to take appropriate measures. He frankly admitted his mistakes to the House, resigned his office and did not seek re-election after the War. Perhaps he didn't mind too much, for he was not merely a politician but that strange creature, commoner then than now, so quaintly called A Man of Letters. Very widely read, he was an accomplished, ironical and amusing reviewer and essayist, remembered today, if at all, for his two volumes of essays entitled *Obiter Dicta*.

Birrell's wife was Eleanor Locker-Lampson, the widow of Tennyson's younger son, Lionel. Birrell told my father that the Laureate wasn't at all pleased when his daughter-in-law wanted to marry a second time. The Birrells had two sons, Francis and Tony. Frankie and his bookshop appear now and then in some of the memoirs of the Bloomsbury Group. He behaved in a superior and supercilious manner to my father who never liked him. Tony was what was then so rightly called simple; today mentally handicapped. Tall, gentle, beautifully mannered, he loved children and was his father's favourite. He was lovingly looked after by a companion-housekeeper, and the last time I saw him, not long after the War, was living in Lyme Regis.

My father's family knew the Birrells because in the early years of the century my restless Ingram grandmother, who was to end up in a villa in St Helena, bought a house near theirs on the cliffs at Sheringham, Norfolk. Like her, the Birrrell's divided their time between London and their Sheringham home, called The Pightle. My father was young then and Birrell was very good to him. He would talk at length about politics, literature, philosophy and his friendship with Browning and Matthew Arnold and before my father went up to Oxford presented him with a fine leatherbound 18th century edition of Johnson's *Shakespeare*.

Time passed. My father married, wrote books himself, had children and lived in his own house not far from The Pightle. A skeptical agnostic, although with a great interest in and understanding of religion, Birrell insisted upon being present at our baptisms even accompanying the godparents, as the custom then was, to the dedication of the child on the Lady altar. In this connection, it was Augustine Birrell who remarked 'It is the Mass that matters' – not his saintly namesake to whom it is sometimes attributed. Birrell was in fact not making a theological statement but putting his finger on one of the cultural differences between Protestantism and Catholicism, England and the Continent.

When he was over eighty Birrell decided to leave Sheringham and to live permanently in Chelsea. Before he left he told my parents that each of us children could take whichever book we pleased from his library. I believe my brother was still at boarding school and so appointed a proxy, nor do I remember what two of my sisters chose. A third sister disgraced herself. Ignoring the books on the shelves, she went straight for an old Harrods Christmas Catalogue which happened to be lying about and obstinately refused to change it for anything else. My father's comments were long and loud. A Harrods Catalogue! The folly of it! A child to choose, might as well ask the cat. Signed copies of the poets, a glorious Dryden, an excellent Pope, a fine Quarles . . .

Hearing the commotion, my mother thought it wise to accompany me to The Pightle herself. To a small child, all grown-ups are huge, very old and to be treated warily. I don't suppose I said anything to Mr Birrell. My mother was far too good mannered to ask for a valuable book but she did not want to disappoint me by choosing something totally unsuitable. She selected a small children's book containing delightful woodcuts called *Goody Two-Shoes* – 'A Facsimile Reproduction of the Edition of 1766 published by Griffith and Farren at the West Corner of St. Paul's Churchyard, 1881'. Inside is written 'Magdalen Watkin from Augustine Birrell, September 1932'. He died a year later.

Don Bradman

by Mike Parton

MY MOTHER HAD gone away for the weekend so my father had no option but to take me to the Woodlands Park Golf Club at Burnham Beeches. 'Stand over there by that tree,' he said on the first tee, 'and don't make a sound.' I was standing under my tree when a butterfly went by. 'Daddy,' I bellowed, 'There's a great big . . . ' My father swung his club and the ball flew into the upper branches of my tree. 'Duck!' he shouted, or at least that's what I thought he shouted at the time.

My father came over to me. 'Look here, Mike,' he said, 'I tell you what, Don Bradman's somewhere over there playing with RWV Robbins. Why don't

you go and ask them to autograph this score card?' I dutifully trotted off.

It took me quite a while to find the celebrated cricketers, but I recognised them easily from the pictures in my cigarette card collection. Don Bradman was standing still, waggling his club over his ball. I ran towards him. 'Sir, please sir!' I yelled, 'Can you please sign my score card please sir?' My hero stopped waggling his club and looked at me. He seemed rather cross. 'You shouldn't do that, son,' he said, 'and anyway I'm off duty on a golf course.' RWV Robbins said nothing.

'Sorry sir,' I said, 'My Daddy said I . . . ' Don Bradman began to smile. 'Do you play cricket?' he asked. 'Oh yes, sir, I'm captain of the Under Tens. I've got a Gun and Moore Autograph bat with three springs.' Bradman patted me on the shoulder.

'Good boy,' he said, 'give us your score card then.' RWV Robbins still didn't say anything.

'Go and stand under that tree, and keep quite still,' he said. He waggled the club again, then hit the ball. 'Keep standing still,' he said. Then RWV Robbins played his shot. It was just like my father's. This time he did say something. It sounded very much like what my father had said.

My father seemed pleased on the way home. When we got back, I put my score card in my toy cupboard.

My mother came home that night and started to tidy up. She was always tidying up. I don't think that she could really help it.

When I got up next morning I went to my toy cupboard to find my score card. The cupboard was very tidy. My dinky toys were all in line. Everything was all in line, but I couldn't find my score card. I never saw it again.

Many years later, after the war, I witnessed Don Bradman's last test innings. As the great man came down the pavilion steps the crowd rose to its feet and clapped him all the way to the wicket. One ball later the stunned crowd rose again and cheered him all the way back. If I'd tried perhaps I could have got him to sign another score card but somehow it didn't seem the right moment.

Sir Matt Busby
by Desmond Albrow

I HAD NO RIGHT to be at such a high-powered lunch, but the Editor of the *Sunday Telegraph* was on holiday and his deputy barely knew the difference between a rugby and a soccer ball, so I was sent off to the rather grand affair celebrating the launch of the World Cup in 1966.

Although soccer had been my game up to about 1943, it had been rugger ever since. At the pre-lunch drinks I was surrounded by the gods of soccer and soccer journalism, who had little to say to an outsider such as me but plenty to say to each other. The lunch itself was set to be, for me, a defensive, plodding business. But it wasn't. It was a sheer delight.

I was seated next to a man who would have been recognisable even if you had never seen a soccer game in your life. He was Matt Busby, the famed survivor of the Munich air disaster that killed so many of his young team almost before they had had a chance to shave. Whether he sensed my unease I don't know, but within moments of introduction he was talking to me as though we were friends of long standing. Paradoxically, it was he who played the journalist, he who was interested in *my* life.

We shared, as it happened, some common ground. I had spent five years on the old *Manchester Guardian* and my son had been born in an Old Trafford hospital. We even touched on religion and discovered that we shared a common faith in Roman Catholicism.

A few days after our meeting there arrived a letter from him enclosing on a separate sheet all the signatures of the Manchester United team, for my son. He had remembered his name correctly. At the time I probably put it down to excellent PR, but after reading his obituaries, I feel it was more than that.

The obituarists portrayed him as a man with a touch of saintliness in a tough and cynical trade. Normally I would not dream of endorsing such comments after a mere three hours in the subject's company. With Sir Matt I make an exception. There was a goodness about him, though not a hint of goodiness.

Mrs Patrick Campbell
by Barbara Ker-Seymer

TO ME SHE looked an ordinary rather stout old woman. She was hard up at the time and reduced to touring the provinces and suburbs with a small company acting the roles she had played when she was young and beautiful. Her company was playing at the King's Theatre, Hammersmith. As we lived nearby, Mother, who though younger than her had been an admirer and longstanding friend, invited her to come to tea and have a rest between the matinée and evening performance, the final one of the season.

Her first words to me were, 'How old are you? What do you do?' I thought she was rather frightening and said timidly that I was nineteen and at art school, and she said, 'When I was your age I was supporting a husband and two children,' which made me feel very inadequate, and I left the room.

When it was time for her to leave, Mother called me and said, 'Mrs Pat wants you to go back to the theatre with her and act as her dresser.' (Her dresser had walked out on her after the matinée, a not unusual occurrence with her dressers, I heard later.) I was very alarmed as I had no idea how to 'dress' an elderly actress. However we went off to the theatre together in a taxi.

I managed to get her out of her dress, to reveal that underneath she was wearing a lace-up corset grey with age, and yellow celanese 'directoire' knickers, the elastic of which, having become slack with age, was tied in a knot at the waist. I managed to get her into her stage costume. There were lots of hooks and eyes in Victorian costumes! She was very preoccupied and taciturn, only speaking to me to bark out instructions. I didn't leave the dressing room when she was on stage and I don't remember what the play was, but it might have been Magda.

For the final act she wore a sequinned evening gown, the sight of which filled me with dismay as there were patches of plain material where sequins had fallen off and strands of black cotton with an odd sequin or two hanging on the end. I didn't know how she dared go on the stage in such a derelict garment. However, I managed to get her into it all right and she left the room.

Some time later I was told the curtain was about to come down, so I crept into the wings. I saw to my amazement a complete transformation had taken place. There in the spotlight stood an elegant and beautiful woman in a shimmering gown, the sequins sparkling in the lights. Bouquets of flowers surrounded her feet, one arm was filled with flowers, the other hand blowing kisses as she bowed and smiled at the audience, who were giving her a standing ovation with tumultuous clapping and cries of 'Bravo! Bravo!'

I was so impressed by this wonderful transformation that I remember it vividly to this day, although it took place nearly 70 years ago.

I never saw her again after that night.

Charlie Chaplin

by James Michie

THURBER, IN HIS piece 'My Memories of D H Lawrence', recorded three conversations with the great writer, though it turned out that in each case he had got the wrong man. My memories of Charlie Chaplin are more authentic; I spent the best part of two days with him at Veyvey in Switzerland, attempting to give him advice on the autobiography he was writing. I was staying at a hotel: I would go to the Chaplin house each day, work with him and eat with the family.

My boss had well-meaningly described me to Chaplin as a distinguished poet and editor. Charlie was a competitive fellow. As soon as he greeted me, spry, fussy, slightly too charming, I saw that here was man physically and metaphorically on the balls of his feet. As soon as we got to work, it was obvious that my role was superfluous – he saw himself not only as an actor, a director and a musician, but as a writer, an editor, possibly something of a poet too. I remember that I suggested he should change the word 'luxurious' to 'luxuriant' in describing some bush in blossom. 'No', he said at once. "Luxurious" sounds much more like a bush. Can't you hear it?' And he read out the sentence both ways, with rich gestures, to prove his point. I appealed to the dictionary. Unluckily, there was a single case of 'luxurious' used in this unusual sense, and, still more unluckily, it was Milton. 'What's good enough for Milton is good enough for me,' he declared. The poet was love-15 down.

And then there was the 'enter' versus 'come in' controversy. Douglas Fairbanks Jnr came into a room in the text. Charlie leapt to his feet. 'That feels all wrong,' he exclaimed. 'Douglas never came into rooms, he *entered* them.' I was more than willing to give in so that we could get on to the next page, but Chaplin was remorseless. He gave one imitation of a person coming into a room, followed by a second, of a person entering a room. 'You see now, don't you, surely?' And to make doubly sure I saw, he insisted that I try coming in and entering myself.

It was quickly game, set and match. Lunch would soon enter or come in. I tried to mime thirst, but my message didn't get through. We worked on after lunch; by mid-afternoon, young and fit though I was, I was exhausted.

I slept well at Les Trois Couronnes that night and woke looking forward to breakfast in a five-star hotel. My telephone rang. It was Chaplin's secretary. Would I go over to the house straight away? Mr Chaplin had been up early reading the typescript with my marked 'corrections' and suggestions, and he was rather upset.

I got through the morning by agreeing with everything he said, an activity which I found even more tiring than the discussions of the day before. Lunch with the family followed. Charlie's conversation reminded me of the famous bread-roll dance in *The Gold Rush* – an utterly self-absorbed performance. His wife, Oonagh, seemed to give him her entire attention; those of his children present shut up and concentrated on the food. His son later wrote a book called *I Couldn't Smoke the Grass on My Father's Lawn*. I know what he meant. And yet, through gritted teeth, I have to admit the little monster was a genius.

Randolph Churchill
by David Ransom

I N A *SUNDAY Telegraph* piece about the rudeness of modern Britons, Peregrine Worsthorne referred to the 'unutterably bad form' of 'lording it' over such people as waiters, shop assistants and the like. He recounted that Randolph Churchill, son of the proper Winston, 'was notoriously prone to "lord it", even over station-masters, and was roundly condemned for his boorishness.' I can confirm this.

As a young man in the late 50s I worked in London during the week, coming home on Friday evening. My father, the parson of a parish near Colchester, would often meet me off the London train. His car was a 1951 black Morris Six, very similar in appearance to those old Wolseley police cars. It was a big car – a sort of Morris major – and at one time it had been used as a taxi. My father, it has to be said, looked more like a taxi driver than a clerk in holy orders. Although he always wore his dog collar he usually wore a sports jacket and flat cap. No black clerical garb for him.

One Friday my father had parked his car immediately outside Colchester station. As I opened the front door of the car, someone came up behind me, pushed me to one side, and throwing open the car's rear door, climbed in and sat down. 'Stour Lodge, driver, and get a move on!' cried the man. I managed to say something like 'I say', before he spoke again. 'Ignore him! Come on, Stour Lodge, East Bergholt!'

My father, who had said nothing, turned round and faced the man, running his finger round his dog-collar. 'Christ Almighty!' said Randolph, for it was he. 'Sorry!' said my father, meekly. 'Only the Rector of Great Bromley, on this occasion.'

Randolph got out and, waving his brolly, yelled 'Taxi! Taxi!' across the station forecourt. By then all the proper taxis had been bagged, and as we drove off he cut a sorry sight standing on the pavement cursing everyone and everything in sight.

Sir Clifford Curzon

by Sophie Radice

ONE SUMMER WHEN I was about ten my friend and I were looking for some amusement. The late Sir Clifford Curzon, pianist and chamber music player, lived next door to her house and each evening he would sit outside with a drink. We decided to ruin his peace and took to slipping into his huge garden and 'streaking' across his lawn at some distance from where he sat.

We imagined that he would rub his eyes in disbelief and look at his drink as if it was responsible for the sight of two naked girls dancing on the grass.

We continued tormenting him, and as my best friend's bedroom window looked over where he sat we decided to hang our repellent-looking teeth-braces out on bits of cotton and dangle them down like glistening clear plastic spiders. When Sir Clifford looked up with surprise and confusion we ducked behind the window, tears of laughter streaming down our faces.

My friend was absolutely mortified when her brace caught in the hedge and fell off. As it had cost a fortune, and she had already lost a good many, she decided that she would rather face the wrath of Sir Clifford than that of her mother.

We rang the door-bell and the butler answered. We explained what had happened, though not quite why we had been hanging our braces out of the window. We waited for a while and almost ran off. Half an hour later the butler returned with a red cushion, upon which sat a revolting plastic brace, two boiled sweets and a little note. The butler smiled and closed the door. We put the sweets in our mouths and walked back into her garden.

The note said: 'Leave me alone, keep your clothes on and no-one shall hear of this. PS. Never accept sweets from strange old men.' We decided from then on that it would be kinder to let him be old in peace.

Diaghilev

by Diana Menuhin

MARIE RAMBERT, MY ballet teacher, had rung my mother with a message: 'Diana is to come to the grown-ups' class tomorrow morning and wear a clean tunic'. To most 14-year-olds, this should have spelt pure bliss. To miss school and join the advanced class, if only for three hours, was surely a heaven-sent exchange. However, in this case, the delight in missing trigonometry was qualified by the penance exacted by Rambert on her pupils, especially me.

Nonetheless, off I went in a whirlwind of excitement and the 31 bus to Notting Hill Gate, to the large Victorian Gothic church hall, which has become the Rambert studio, and which, with its smelly anthracite stove, added a further touch of purgatory to the pursuit of classic dance. Heartened by the delight that a break in routine will bring the young, and still living in those clouds of rapture Rambert's acerbic tongue had not yet dispersed, I never thought to question why I had had this honour conferred upon me, nor why the other dancers looked as though they had come by tumbril.

Out to the barre we trouped and to the inevitable barrage that awaited us. The out-of-tune upright banged away at its uninspiring scraps of popular operetta while we slogged and tugged, doggedly absorbing Rambert's discouragements. I had just turned, and was facing the door, when it opened. There, perfectly fitted in its Gothic frame like some idol, obsidian eyes set in the pouch of an ashen face, the white streak like a stilled flash of lightning marking the black hair, stood Sergei Pavlovich Diaghilev, his hands folded over his silver-knobbed cane. Stood, in fact, God. My heart went once right round my body, and I was in flight, levitated by the shock his presence brought. A world of time later, I alighted to find myself quite alone in the studio, being asked whether I would dance one of the Variations from 'Casse Noisette'. I complied with the 'Carnation Fairy', curtsied and retreated to the empty dressing room, still in a state of artless fuddle.

I had taken off one shoe when there was a knock. Hobbling to the door, I opened it to see Diaghilev standing there. Cupping a hand under my chin he told me in his romantic Slav French that I was to join his company the following autumn. Meanwhile he would give me two seats for every ballet performance that final week of the season and introduce me to all the dancers – 'Parce que' he said, turning to Rambert, 'je voudrais leur présenter la seule jeune fille que je voudrais épouser.'

It was the most magical week of my life. He died ten days before I was due to join.

Jean Manuel Fangio
by Charles Lucas

IN 1965 I was running an enthusiastic but not very professional Formula 3 team with my dear friend Piers Courage (d Zandvoort 1971) and Jonathan Williams (*vivant* St Tropez), when life seemed to come in small bytes of pure joy as we hurried round Europe from one provincial race track to the next with our low-tech Ford-engined Brabham cars.

So it came as no surprise when we were invited to go to the Argentine to run in the Temporada Series by Fangio's erstwhile manager, Enrico Vanini. We had been selected, Enrico said, and we had been offered especially favourable terms, Enrico said, because Fangio wanted us to take a car over to run for his son, Cacho. When God calls, do you check the small print?

So we packed the cars up and sailed away, and Fangio met us, and he was generous and charming; his business associate and former team mate, Froilan Gonzales (the Pampas Bull) marginally less so. And with the same mesmeric slate blue eyes, Cacho was certainly a son of the Great Man; (there were, apparently, not a few, though there appeared to be no Mrs Fangio).

Unfortunately Cacho couldn't drive for toffee. He was, of course, in an impossible situation, being who he was, and trying to compete with these professional Europeans in a strange car – as his father well knew – and it was only a matter of time before he wrecked the car against a lamp post in the crowded and cobbled streets of Rosario. And Fangio was so charming and so *simpatico*, and of course the damage would be paid for . . . *mañana*.

I later realised, of course, that he was also eternally grateful as the wretched Cacho had, relatively painlessly – and at no cost to himself – been persuaded that racing was not for him, and when I finally returned to our garage in Highgate with the debris after the series (Piers had also wiped out a car at Buenos Aires), I did receive a signed photograph and a letter of thanks from Fangio, which I treasure to this day.

Many years later I met him again when he was the guest of honour at the Nürburgring, and I was racing an old 250F Maserati which he had driven to one of his memorable victories at Monaco in 1957. He came over, shook me warmly by the hand and said, in his small Spanish, what I took to mean, 'This is one of my greatest friends.' As my heart swelled with pride, the translator explained that he was, of course, talking about the car.

E M Forster

by Nonie Beerbohm

ONE BRIGHT SUNNY day many years ago when I was living and teaching in Bishop's Stortford, a pretty young friend invited me to drive into Cambridge with her to do some essential shopping. Her doctor husband was driving and, as parking was a problem, he put us down on the Backs and suggested that we should walk through the precincts of King's College into King's Parade.

My friend put her small son into the smallest of pushchairs and we passed through the massive gate. As we walked along the path we admired the beauty of the ancient lawn and the splendour of King's College Chapel in the sunlight. It was all so beautiful.

Suddenly the peace was destroyed by someone shouting 'Get back! Go away! How dare you!' I looked behind me to see if rowdy students were making a disturbance – and realised that we were the cause of this outburst of rage. A small, frantic old man in a long overcoat, cap and scarf was scuttling down the steps of an adjacent building, waving his stick in a threatening manner at us – two astonished young women and a startled baby.

'Can you not read?' he screeched. 'Do you not read notices? You are not allowed in these precincts with a *perambulator!*'

I could read. I had recognised this angry little figure at once as Edward Morgan Forster. I had read all his books with great pleasure ('Only connect' his salient message).

I was not easily intimidated. Did I not deal with students every day of the week? My gentle friend was pink with embarrassment and totally silenced. I was not.

I said quietly: 'Do calm down or you will have a stroke.'

His mouth fell open in amazement and his entire manner changed. He said quite politely: 'You are not allowed in here with a *wheeled* vehicle. There is a notice on the gate. You must go back.' I replied: 'We are within a few yards of King's Parade and quite some distance from the gate through which we entered. Should we not wheel this small pushchair through the nearest exit?' 'Go on then,' he muttered, 'and don't do it again!'

I wish I had never met that most sensitive of writers, E M Forster.

John Galsworthy

by Jean MacGibbon

WHEN I WAS nineteen I was sent to my uncle and aunt in Mombasa to get over an unsuitable liaison. From there I wrote to John Galsworthy telling him what it was I admired about his books. At that time, in the early Thirties, he was a literary giant – a Nobel Prize winner, his work established as a modern classic, revered at home and abroad. So when his reply arrived I hastened to read it under my mosquito net on the verandah. My letter, he wrote, was the kind authors most like getting. Our correspondence continued. When I returned home, finding we lived near by, I wrote asking myself to tea.

'Ah,' he replied, 'that way disillusion lies!' I went all the same, wearing a tweed suit the colour of grass in spring, with astrakhan revers the colour of a brown spaniel, and a bowler hat to match with a small green and scarlet bird over one eye. His house, appropriately, was just below the great Admiral's House on one of Hampstead's literary and artistic hills immortalised by Constable. He opened the door himself, accompanied by a medium-sized dog. He was tall, serenely handsome with clear-cut features, wearing an old-fashioned stiff collar under his noble chin. Our tea was a tête-à-tête – his wife, he apologised, was lying down, they had just crossed the Channel. (Ah, I thought, Irene!) He offered me a scone.

Mr Galsworthy had been right. We had nothing to exchange. We never got on to books or discussed *The Forsyte Saga*, just re-issued complete in one volume. I had no opportunity to tell him I had translated *The Inn of Tranquillity* into French. Early on he asked if I liked dogs? I didn't, and my pretence was hollow. After a polite interval he asked me to excuse him, he ought to go up and see his wife. I wondered if he had liked my hat. From time to time he had given it a fixed stare, then looked away. Perhaps, I thought, he too had been sick on the Channel.

How long did it take me to work out that above all things, even above cruelty to women, he hated cruelty to animals? No doubt it was in his mind that astrakhan was stripped from live lambs. I could have told him the bird on my hat was not a real bird.

Robert Graves

by John Mortimer

I ONCE MET ROBERT Graves. He was old, I don't know how old, but eternally handsome, grey-haired and he sat like an emperor on a sofa beside me and said, 'Jesus Christ, of course, lived to the age of 80, when he went to China and discovered spaghetti.' Someone else, so far as I can remember it was Jo Grimond, was also on the sofa with us. Mr Graves had puzzled him. 'Which Gospel is it exactly,' he asked politely, 'in which we read that Jesus went to China and discovered spaghetti?' 'It's not in a Gospel,' Graves answered with imperious simplicity. 'It's a well-known fact of history.'

Later I said, 'We all remember what you did in the 1914 war, but what did you do in the last war?' 'I won the Battle of Anzio,' he told me. 'How did you manage that?' 'Well, I was cycling round the island of Jersey during the War and I met an officer in my old regiment, the Welsh Guards. I asked him what he was doing and he said, "We're off the fight the Eyeties." So I said, "I'll think of a plan by which you can beat the Eyeties." So I cycled round the island again and when I got back to him I said, "There's one thing that really scares an Eyetie and that is the cry of a woman in labour. So you want to go to Queen Charlotte's Hospital and record all the women in labour, then play their cries on gramophones to the Eyeties and they'll run a mile." Well, that's exactly what happened and so we won the Battle of Anzio. Records of women in labour were playing all along the beaches.'

I had adapted *I Claudius* and *Claudius the God* – two books to which I had long been devoted – for the stage, and the play was directed by Tony Richardson, in whose house I met Robert Graves. To ensure the play's success he had brought a fragment of meteorite which he held in his hand. 'How will you get it to bring us good notices and a long run?' I asked him. 'I shall simply say to it: "Magic stone, do your job!".' Perhaps it was the wrong formula, for the stone went off-duty on the first night and the play was a flop. But I shall always remember, with joy, discussing the well known facts of history on a sofa with Robert Graves.

Graham Greene
by John Chilton

URING THE EARLY 1970s, quite soon after my wife achieved her ambition of owning a second-hand bookshop, she took maternity leave. I temporarily gave up the life of a travelling jazz musician to look after the enterprise (in London WC1). Customers were few and far between. In a way this was fortunate because the premises were so tiny that any more than three browsers at a time and the place was packed.

The dimensions made it impossible not to be aware of a customer entering the shop. Usually I looked up from whatever I was reading and atttempted a smile, but on one particular morning I was so engrossed in a book-trade magazine that I didn't even glance at the newcomer. The article which so intrigued me was by a bookseller who described a frosty encounter he'd had with Graham Greene. I finished the piece then glanced at my solitary visitor. It was Graham Greene.

I stared disbelievingly at the tall figure and let out an involuntary grunt of amazement. This caused a pair of watery, but vividly blue eyes to focus on me in a way that seemed to demand an explanation for the ugly sound.

'You won't believe this, Mr Greene, but I was jut reading an account of you visiting a small second-hand bookshop and I look up and here you are.' He gave rather a wan smile as I backed up my story by waving the magazine at him.

'Yes, I've read that, but naturally I viewed the incident rather differently.'

I was completely nonplussed. The publication had only arrived that morning. Was the great man's reading list so extensive that he'd already found time to take in the contents of a small circulation trade journal? Apparently so, because he went on to give his own amusing description of his visit to the bookshop.

He talked about living in Bloomsbury years before. He didn't visit the area often but was doing so in order to see a friend who was a patient in the nearby Italian Hospital. He spotted a book, *Where Black Rules White,* and this led him on to discussing Haiti. I mentioned Haitian music and he gave a marvellous account of being kept awake by a band on the outskirts of Port-au-Prince.

I wanted to make a gift of the book he'd chosen, *Ezra Pound in Kensington,* but he insisted on paying for it. I pulled a copy of *Our Man in Havana* from a shelf and asked if he'd mind signing it. He asked my name and wrote a warm inscription. I thanked him and mentioned film criticism, which led to him reeling off a string of yesteryear stars, including Harold Lloyd. I commented that Lloyd had named one of his characters Harold Diddlebock only to find that real Mr H D had jumped up and demanded an apology. Greene smiled and said, 'I always make a special point of avoiding any name that might be recognised.'

We shook hands and he buttoned his excessively long black overcoat and left. Some while later I read Greene's novel *The Human Factor* and saw that the author had named a character (who appears once) Chilton.

Sir Alec Guinness

by O F Snelling

THE OCCASION WAS a sale by auction of rare books – mostly modern first editions and private press volumes – at Sotheby's popular Chancery Lane rooms, in the late 1970s. I was officiating at the desk beside the rostrum, and after about 30 years' experience in the book trade, I knew – at least by name or face – quite nine-tenths of the 'groundlings' sitting or standing below me. Not so the auctioneer who was conducting the sale.

A private press edition of one of Shakespeare's plays came up for sale. I can't remember which one it was now. As I recall it was a handsomely printed tome, bound in green.

Bidding was brisk, and I noticed, in the far left-hand corner of the room, that one of the competitors was a rather ordinary looking gentleman, very soberly-dressed in a dark blue overcoat.

Being something of a film buff, I caught on to those features immediately, and I watched with interest as the bidding went back and forth. Finally, down came the hammer with a bang, and at a very respectable price. But to my amazement, the auctioneer called one of the well-known London booksellers as the purchaser! I never saw a face drop so far as that of that 'ordinary' punter at the far end of the room. And it was here that I stepped in.

'Oh,' I said to the auctioneer, 'Sir Alec was bidding.'

If I'd said that Alf Bloggs had been bidding, I doubt if it would have made much difference. But the title I mentioned had made a great deal. The lot was put up again, but the dealer had reached his limit. The Shakespeare went to the chap in the far corner.

'Sir Alec Guinness,' I called loudly, since nobody else, including the man selling, seemed to be aware of who the buyer was. Naturally, there was a muttering, and a slight turning of heads, but I then forgot all about it and concentrated on the many lots to come before this auction was over.

Some short while later, a modest figure put in a quiet appearance beside me at the desk. Sir Alec nodded gratefully, and thanked me for intervening on his behalf. He paid me for his purchase, which he was obviously very happy to have made, I receipted his bill, he collected the book from the porter, and departed – blue overcoat, black bowler hat, et al.

Dr Kurt Hahn

by Walter Kelly

‘THE FOUNDER’ WAS a remote, already legendary figure by the time I arrived at Gordonstoun in 1953. Indeed, his status and his whereabouts were a mystery. It was rumoured that when he was stricken by a brain tumour, the governors had given up on him and appointed his successor.

But Hahn was nothing if not unpredictable. Upon receiving this news, he rose from his death-bed incandescent, and demanded instant reinstatement! Whilst the governors brooded over their embarrassment, the school revelled in the drama and suspense.

Sightings of the great man were a rarity. Once his enormous solar topee, which it was claimed he even wore in bed, was spotted bobbing around the grounds, and the word flew around 'He's back! He's back' – but he vanished again.

One drowsy summer's afternoon, I was told to practise the high jump and left to my own devices. Within a few minutes I was asleep in the long grass by the pit. Suddenly a window in the main building shot up, and an unmistakable voice boomed out 'Hello there, my man! Why are you resting? Stay there! I am coming!' I scrambled to my feet, but before I could escape he was bounding over the grass towards me.

'Are you ill, my man? No! Why do you not jump then? No-one teaches you. Very well then, I will teach you!'

He proceeded to give me the most exacting lesson – Scissors, Western roll, even an attempt at Straddle – the sweat poured off me in fear and exhilaration. I jumped far higher than I had ever dared before, but still he raised the bar, and demanded more and more effort.

Angry faces appeared at the window, and angry voices called out 'Dr Hahn, you have a meeting!' 'Dr Hahn, we are waiting for you!' 'Really, Dr Hahn!' 'Dr Hahn!'

He ignored them for what seemed like an age, until with a sigh he bowed his head, gave me a most formal handshake, and turned wearily back to the building.

The meeting must have been amongst the last he was called to for he never appeared at the school again.

Later I was told that he had once held the world Standing High Jump record. Alas, I never had a chance to ask him.

Oscar Hammerstein
by Douglas Sutherland

IT WAS IN the early 1950s when the musicals of Rogers and Hammerstein were bringing a new vitality to the war-tired London stage. He had invited my wife and me to lunch with him at the Caprice restaurant, then London's most 'in' place for show-business folk. My own circumstances at the time were not nearly so glamorous. I too was rather war-tired and had recently undergone treatment for the dispersal of gastric ulcers. Thus I found myself seated in the cocktail bar at the Caprice gazing moodily at a glass of tonic water.

Hammerstein himself arrived before my wife, looking like a cross between a bare-fist fighter and an ageing all-America quarterback, his grey hair cut *en brosse* after the then-prevailing transatlantic fashion.

'Whassat your drinking?' he demanded. I told him somewhat shamefacedly, and added that it was on medical advice.

'Sounds to me like the usual load of crap,' he said and, ordering himself a large something-or-other, proceeded to apply himself with flattering attention to my case history.

'Waal,' he said at last, with a touch of world-weariness, 'I sure cured Richard Rogers and I guess I'm gonna cure you.' A page boy was sent for. 'Go to the nearest chemist,' the great man instructed him, 'and buy the largest size of soluble capsule which they have in stock. On the way back stop and purchase a packet of Dreft washing powder.'

When the page returned with the required items, Oscar Hammerstein II filled one of the capsules with the then newly-marketed miracle washing powder and, handing it to me, commanded that I swallow it.

'Take one every morning for a while and you should be fine,' he proscribed with the air of a trusted family doctor. 'Now you can have some gin in that tonic water.'

I did as I was told and I must report that, although for some time afterwards bubbles came out of my ears whenever I blew my nose, I have never suffered from any more ulcer trouble, for going on 40 years.

Oliver Hardy
by George Macdonald Fraser

I KNEW OLIVER HARDY for all of five minutes, and never met a kinder or more courteous man, despite the fact that I'd walked in on him unannounced after a long and tiring performance in which he and Stan Laurel, old troupers at the end of their careers, had worked their hearts out in a small provincial theatre. Although I was a young newspaperman at the time, I had no thought of an interview; I just wanted to meet an immortal.

In the mid-50s, when Laurel and Hardy made their last British tour, they were the penultimate act on a variety bill at Her Majesty's, Carlisle. They were old men now, supposedly past it, and the audience was prepared to be critical. 'They reckon Laurel an' 'Ardy spoil this show,' a red-faced man told the Gents' with grim Cumbrian satisfaction; fifteen minutes later I watched him doubled up and apoplectic with laughter as the two great men appeared from opposite wings and performed that brilliant routine in which neither sees the other, turning in bewilderment behind each other's backs with a speed and perfection of timing that would have graced a ballet.

On an impulse I went backstage during the last act. There were two doors labelled 'Stan Laurel' and 'Oliver Hardy'. I chose Hardy's without hesitation, knocked, heard the well-known voice call 'Come in!', and there he was, sitting four-square, bowler on head, hands on knees, wearing that familiar look of weary resignation. I apologised for intruding, and he smiled and waved me to a seat.

'I just wanted to say thank you, Mr Hardy, for everything,' I said, fairly lamely, and he said: 'You're Scottish,' adding that so was he, by descent (and years later I thought of him when I heard Steve McQueen, with precisely the same tilt of the head and quiet satisfaction, announce: 'I'm Scotch.')

Having got in, I was in haste to get out again, for he looked tired, and I'd no wish to be a nuisance, but he reminisced amiably about 'Bonnie Scotland' and 'Putting Pants on Philip', and the happy memories he and 'Stanley' had of Edinburgh and Glasgow.

At last I got up, and thanked him again. 'Thank you,' he said. 'Good of you to drop in. God bless.' We shook hands, and as I reached the door he said 'Hey' softly, and I looked back. He was sitting there, beaming, in the bowler and the baggy suit, and I realised he was giving me the Hardy farewell that all the world remembers: flapping his tie at me with his fingers.

Hitler

by Humphrey ap Evans

I N 1936, MY adored elder brother died after a car smash, a Lea Francis in which he had declared his intention of entering a Grand Prix and becoming a racing driver. If I had been with him, I suppose I would have been dead too. But I was in bed with German measles, so missed it all. To alleviate my trauma, my world having unbelievably collapsed at the age of thirteen, my parents took me to Germany to shoot a Chamois – guns and hunting were my passion. A family acquaintance lived in a tiny medieval Schloss in the foothills, bare stone walls throughout the interior, servant girls in what seemed to be gaily embroidered fancy dress, massive wooden tables in the white-painted dining hall, and pewter bowls and plates everywhere. One evening at dinner, a uniformed Keeper hurried in, ashen-faced, and whispered to our host. He rose at once from the table and announced: 'Will everyone please go at once to your rooms and remain there.' Consternation ensued among the twenty or so diners, but in view of the evident urgency of this sudden and unexplained request, everyone filed dutifully away. Except for me. I slid behind a screen and made my way down the kitchen stairs and through to the front courtyard. My German was passable. 'What's happening?' I asked. Nobody would answer. Outside the gatehouse were several large black cars. Round them stood some uniformed men carrying what looked like interesting weapons, such as I had not seen before. I went to ask one of them about his pistol, but he paid no attention to me. Suddenly, a car door opened and a small man in a dark shirt lent out. Everyone snapped to attention. He said some thing I did not understand, pointing at me. 'Oh, excuse me, Sir,' I said in careful, if hesitant German, but very polite all the same, 'I wanted to see this pistol.' The small man laughed loud and short, clapped me on the shoulder, and slammed the door. Someone pulled me away and I was escorted up to my parents' room. 'What on earth have you been doing? It's the Secret Police.'

After the place had calmed down and the car loads of police had gone away, I became a minor hero. 'What did Hitler say to you?' 'Hitler? Oh Hitler, yes . . . Was *that* Hitler?'

After getting so warmly acquainted with the great man, I wrote to him from school but he never replied. Rather a swizz.

Jack Hobbs
by Winefride Pruden

I DON'T KNOW IF I was ever wheeled into Lords or the Oval in my pram, but I cannot remember a time when I was not taken to cricket matches. I watched Larwood bowl and Bradman bat, and I saw Chapman lead out his team, wearing a silk shirt which billowed in the breeze, and blue socks.

When choosing a school for me, my father's priorities were cricket and Latin, probably in that order. Patsy Hendren was our coach at one time, but

Hobbs was my hero. He must have been in his late forties by the time I first saw him, but he could still play any stroke on any wicket with consummate artistry and grace. His perfect partner was Sutcliffe, with whom he used to sneak such witty singles that the spectators laughed as well as applauded. But this was not all. His combination of mastery and modesty was unique. His goodness shone out almost visibly like an aureole around him: as John Arlott said, 'If he had never scored a run or excelled at any sport, those who knew him must have seen him as a great man, because of the unmistakable nobility of his character.'

He retired while I was still only a schoolgirl, but his performances remained etched on my memory, and every subsequent batsman whom I saw was weighed in the balance and found wanting. I was not an autograph-hunter, and I never tried to waylay him as he left the pavilion. But now you must imagine one of those film clichés in which the pages of a calendar are rapidly turned, or trees bud and instantly shed their leaves, to indicate the passage of time. Cut to 1963.

I was waiting in a queue at Hove Post Office one day when I became aware of a tall, lean old man in a long, dark overcoat standing just in front of me. The counter-clerk was checking the number of words in a telegram, and when he said, 'That comes to nine pounds, sir', the old man exclaimed, 'I say, that's rather a lot, isn't it?' 'Well, let's see if we can cut it down a bit', suggested the clerk; and he proceeded to read aloud the text of the message, expertly translating it into telegramese. In this way, I learned that its purpose was to congratulate the MCC team, who had achieved a notable victory in New Zealand.

I knew that Hobbs in his retirement lived in a flat overlooking the Hove cricket ground, and a sly peep at the old man's profile assured me that it was indeed he. 'How's that, sir? I've got it down to six pounds ten,' said the clerk triumphantly. I followed Hobbs to the door, my own errand forgotten. 'Oh, Sir Jack,' I burbled like a starstruck teenager, 'I'm so glad to have this opportunity of telling you that you've given me more pleasure in my life than anyone except John Gielgud!' (My husband was not there to overhear this.) A tear trickled down the old man's cheek. 'Thank you,' he said with a gentle smile. 'They were great days.'

A few months later, he was dead. He had nursed his wife through a long illness, and when she died he was like the subject of Henry Wotton's verse:

> *She first deceased. He for a little tried*
> *To live without her: liked it not, and died.*

Ronny Kray
by Keri Spencer

AGED EIGHTEEN AND straight out of boarding school, I found myself in 1964 sharing a London flat with a girl of a similar background, but with an astonishing facility for knowing someone who knew someone who . . . well, absolutely anything!

When Christine Keeler emerged from prison and took up residence across the road, I was not surprised that my gregarious flatmate soon took up her acquaintance. I have to say that I felt a twinge of envy and hoped, vainly, for an invitation.

One evening, however, I arrived at our 'pad' to find my friend looking rather apprehensive and being excessively considerate – not her usual style – to an enormous and distinctly not-our-kind-of person whom she had met across the road. A weaselly looking fellow was hovering, lighting his cigarettes and filling his glass. He appeared to be perfectly at home. I hoped it was not my scotch he was enjoying.

'He's staying a few days,' she murmured.

'No he's bloody not,' said I breezily, avoiding his steely gaze. 'No room. Terribly sorry.'

'I am Ronnie Kray,' the gimlet-eyed visitor announced in a definitive and dismissive sort of way.

'Well,' I riposted. 'What an elegant name! Still no room, old thing.'

'You,' he growled, 'are an *iggerant* bitch.'

'No, no, dear,' I told this fearsome-looking character, straight out of the less PC fairy tales, 'the word is I-G-N-O-R-A-N-T. Sorry, but I'm sure someone of your charm will soon get fixed up.' And with that, I tootled out to meet a friend.

Half way up the road, the weasel caught up with me. 'I just said I was nipping out for a packet of fags,' he gasped in pure theatrical Cockney tones. 'Haven't you heard of him? Don't you realise that you've *annoyed* him?'

'So?'

'So, you'll find yourself propping up a bridge on the M1 if you ever go back to your flat. He just puts people like you into concrete mixers.' For the first time I was afraid.

I met my friend and stayed there. When two trusty pals went into my flat the next day, they found two large, unattractive thugs in my bedroom.

'Where is she?'

'Don't know,' they muttered. 'We just popped in for a few bits of her room-mate's, who's in hospital.'

They grabbed as much as they could and fled. I never went back.

Philip Larkin

by Glyn Lloyd

I N 1928 I was a six year old pupil at Cheshunt School, Manor Road, Coventry. This was a preparatory school for girls but it also accepted boys at kindergarten level. The school was a converted suburban house with ample garden and extra classrooms built on, and was owned and run by the Miss Bottomleys (Miss Ethel and Miss Evelyn). One day, as I remember it was mid-term, a new boy arrived. Not yet possessing a school uniform, he was conspicuous in a sailor suit and flat sailor hat, complete with ribbon and *HMS Pinafore* in gold letters across the front. This was Philip Larkin. We were the same age, in the same form together, and naturally became friends.

I remember Philip at school entertaining us during morning breaks with stories accompanied by illustrations on the blackboard. These were humorous, often with a strong excremental bias and therefore guaranteed to get a laugh from six-year-old boys. (I recall one vivid drawing of an aircraft crashing into the local sewage works.) On Saturdays we would play football together with other little boys in our road. Philip was a goalkeeper of moderate ability, but was handicapped at ball games by his myopia, which I don't think was then recognised.

Senior Oldies will perhaps recall the importance of cigarette-card collecting to schoolboys in the period between the wars. Most fathers and uncles smoked Players Navy Cut or Wills Goldflake. There was little to choose between the two brands, and I would encourage my father to alternate according to which set of cards I happened to be collecting. The competition to be the first in the school with a complete set was intense, especially if footballers or cricketers were the subject of the series.

In late 1929 or early 1930 a new series of cards was issued consisting of international rugby footballers. I had collected about half the set and kept the cards in an album specially designed for them. One day when I was about to add new cards to my collection, I discovered that at least half were missing. I was distraught and let out a bellow of tearful rage, alerting the rest of the family to the situation. Circumstantial evidence pointed to Philip as prime suspect.

My mother was emphatic: he had been looking through the album only recently when on a lunchtime visit.

How to obtain proof or, more importantly, retrieve the cards was another matter. The family were sympathetic but perhaps did not appreciate the full magnitude of my loss. My best friend Peter, who was also collecting the series, was more understanding. He was nearly a year older and, at the age of eight and a half, capable of righteous indignation. He overcame my diffidence and together we called at the Larkin house, accusing Philip of taking the cards, and demanding them back. He did return them. Unfortunately they had been defaced: all the beautiful red, white, blue and green shirts had been obliterated beneath a pattern of fine cross-hatching in blue-black ink! Decades later, in memorable English, Philip laid much blame on his mum and dad. I wouldn't know about that; but certainly in terms of f—king things up, he did a Grade A job on my cigarette cards.

The Last Squire of Erddig

by Michael Strachan

MY WIFE AND I visited Erddig near Wrexham not long after the great house had been donated to the National Trust. One enters the house via the kitchen, where we found a small, sandy-haired man in a crumpled suit becoming increasingly frustrated through not getting the better of a clockwork roasting spit from which a stuffed pheasant was suspended. My wife eventually offered to show him how it worked, for which he was courteously grateful. We resumed our tour of the house. 'And this,' said our guide, 'is a portrait of the last Squire of Erddig,' at which the sandy-haired man poked his head round the door, and we recognised who he was.

He appeared again as we were about to leave, so we told him how much we had enjoyed our visit. 'Where are you from?' he asked. 'Scotland,' we replied. 'Ah, do you know David Baird?' 'We know a David Baird, but . . .' 'Wait a jiffy,' he said and trotted off, returning with a snapshot. Seated in a coxless two-oared sculling boat were the diminutive figure of himself and the very large David Baird we knew. It transpired that they, and I from a later date, were all old members of the same Cambridge college. After that he insisted we should spend the night with him, rather than at a hotel. It was agreed that we should give him dinner. 'I know a very good restaurant,' he said. 'I'll just get my bike.' He refused to be helped to load it onto our roof rack, and the roof received a grievous dent.

What we had envisaged as a comfortable dower house nearby, turned out to be a remote row of three labourers' cottages. The centre one was occupied by the last Squire, the two adjoining were derelict. The little gardens had been neglected for a very long time. 'I shall get all this tidied up next week,' he said. Inside the front door stood a large table with scores of unopened letters, gathering dust. Dust was everywhere. He brought his bike inside, we left our bags and all drove off in search of dinner.

We motored through the countryside for some miles and eventually came to a house with its windows boarded up. 'Oh dear,' he said, 'I am afraid the restaurant has closed down. Never mind, I know another very good one.' So we drove on through the dusk until we arrived in a village and stopped outside a house with a light in the window. 'I'll just go in and make sure we're not too late,' he said. After a longish wait he reappeared. 'I'm so sorry, his wife says he's inside again.'

After that we insisted on driving to a large hotel. 'I only eat food mentioned in the Bible,' he said; but he managed a hearty meal of fish and fruit washed down with plenty of white wine. Over dinner he told us more about his life. At Cambridge he had formed his own theatre company and after Cambridge had taken it on tour in a bus. The bus broke down at Bexhill-on-Sea, so they stayed there for a year or so until the company disintegrated. He had been a tourists' courier in Spain, was something of an authority on that country and gave lectures about it. He was also a lay preacher.

When he inherited Erddig from his elder brother he had squatted in the great house while it became more and more dilapidated. Finally he had removed the burden of ownership by giving the whole property to the National Trust. Now a major occupation was criticising the Trust's actions. He had added to his lecturing repertoire 'my Anti-National Trust Lecture'.

Back at this cottage: 'Here's your room – my last visitor was a tinker – splendid fellow, but needed a bath. The lights don't work very well – I could try to rig something up with this flex – ' starting to climb on a chair. We implored him not to trouble, got as quickly as possible between the purple sheets, and were thoroughly flea-bitten.

Some weeks later we read that while delivering a sermon from the pulpit he had suffered a heart attack and died.

L S Lowry
by A N Wilson

I CALLED, UNANNOUNCED, at the house of L S Lowry when I was aged 12, and he was – what? – 70 odd. 'Bob a job?' No thanks. You want what?' I was holding a small portfolio of paintings and drawings to show him. 'You want to be a painter? Better come in.'

Outside, the house was coal-black. Inside was chaos. A back room, from whose ceiling a bare 100-watt bulb dangled, served as a studio. Canvases were leaning everywhere. Paint dribbled down the edge of the easel. The floor was strewn with tubes of more-or-less empty Flake white.

'What do you want to know?'

Having been bold enough to visit the famous artist, I did not have the courage to follow it up with any interesting questions. He resumed work on a painting. It was a seascape – streaks of white and grey. No figures, almost no colour. Just mist. 'I go more and more to Sunderland. I like the sea. And I'll let you into a secret about why I like painting either houses and streets or the sea. I can't draw trees at all. Never could. Another reason I go to the seaside so much these days is that I hate this house. Always have done. An absolutely horrible house.' For a while he daubed in silence. I asked an idiot school boy question – 'I wonder how many tubes of white paint you have got through in the course of your life?' '

'Now if you become a painter, you won't find it easy to make money. By no means!'

His face came very close to mine. I was struck by its prison pallor, and the very bright blue eyes and by the white hair *en brosse*, like a polar bear's.

Insensitively, I hung around for hours. He made me tea. Then he went and changed from his paint-spattered suit to a clean one, and placed a hat on his head—a trilby whose crown he had carefully punched out to make it the shape of a bowler.

He told me that he would escort me back to Manchester, presumably the only way he could think of getting rid of me.

'Thank you, sir' – this to the bus conductor who gave us our tickets. Then, to me, 'Do you enjoy music? Which composers?' I said Schubert. 'Well, you could do much worse than Schubert. I like to listen to the gramophone while I'm working. Now the difference between an artist and everyone else is that everyone else is only happy when they stop working, an artist is only happy when he *is* working. But oh, it does make me tired. Do you see that wall? I once saw a man lying on top of that wall. I did a painting of it. Oh, yes, I'm tired. Want to go back to the seaside.'

Mr Lowry had spent the better part of a day with me, and delivered me to my mother, who was having tea in one of the larger department stores – Marshall and Snelgrove, I think. When he had gone, I realised that I had left my small portfolio of paintings and drawings behind at his house. I would never have dared to go back for them.

Hugh MacDiarmid
by Michael Strachan

THE SPECULATIVE SOCIETY, whose anteroom, debating hall and library are just inside the entrance to Old Court, within but not part of Edinburgh University, was founded in 1764 'for the Improvement of Literary Composition and Public Speaking'. Its members have included Sir Walter Scott and R L Stevenson, Lord Brougham and Lord John Russell, Prince Alfred Duke of Edinburgh and Prince William of Hesse (both great-uncles of Prince Philip), many luminaries of the Scottish legal profession, some of the medical profession, and a few 'industrials' – like me.

In the later 40s, when I was elected, few Speculators had a taste for Hugh MacDiarmid's writings, and fewer if any were in sympathy with his political views. Times change; by 1964 when the Society celebrated its bicentenary with a grand banquet he had become a celebrity, a national figure, and had been elected the Society's Honorary Bard.

At the banquet he was invited, because of a known tendency to become less coherent during the course of an evening, to declaim after the first course from a central position at the high table. His brilliant contribution, partly in verse, partly in prose, was loudly applauded as he resumed his place on the outermost sprig at which I sat a few places away.

Dinner proceeded, after which the Duke of Edinburgh, an Honorary Member, rose to speak. Scarcely had he begun than H MacD started to interject: 'Nonsense! . . . What's he saying? . . . Never heard such rubbish' etc, etc. Prince Philip weathered all this with good humour. Shortly afterwards the Honorary Bard lapsed into silence, then fell off his chair and lay prostrate.

I and another member, who was medically qualified, rushed to assist him. The doctor, having quickly ascertained that there was no cause for particular alarm, took the legs, I took the shoulders and we carried the little body through an adjacent side exit. Just outside this, a large empty laundry hamper was ready to receive the evening's napery, so we popped him in to sleep it off, returned to our places and listened to the rest of the proceedings, which had continued uninterrupted.

The Honorary Bard suffered no ill effects and lived to write, rant and drink until his eighty-sixth year.

Harpo Marx
by Selwyn Powell

I WAS ON *Picture Post* at the time, editing the so-called funny page, or rather, preparing specimen funny pages to show what they could be like. I had at my disposal any number of artists and writers to help me, including Patrick Campbell, then on the staff of *Lilliput* (like *Picture Post* one of the Hulton group). Harpo Marx was in London, making a personal appearance at the Palace Theatre in a variety show. He appeared, dressed as usual in his shaggy wig of red hair and capacious, shapeless garments straight from a rag-bag. He played his harp: serious music, beautifully performed. We all applauded loudly; Harpo came forward to the front of the stage to acknowledge the applause. He bowed, and as he did so a spoon dropped out of a sleeve. He looked embarrassed. A couple more dropped from the other sleeve, and then more. Spoons and

knives and forks, clattering in a cascade from his garments, each offering making him more and more embarrassed. It was astounding. He stood ankle-deep in the things. How on earth he had played the harp, and so well, for so long, while carrying such a weight of cutlery no-one will ever know. It was incredibly, earth-shakingly funny.

We cut here to Harpo's bedroom at the Savoy. (I was a bit disappointed at the ordinariness of a Savoy bedroom). How I got there is as mysterious as the spoons and forks disgorged by Harpo on the Palace Theatre stage. I had recently been to the National Gallery and had noticed the astonished likeness of one of the figures in a Rubens painting to Harpo. When shown a photograph of the painting, Harpo agreed. In real life, small, bald and very Jewish, he was a man you wouldn't notice on a bus or in a supermarket. He was wearing an open-necked shirt and ordinary trousers. At once he put on the magic wig. Somehow his eyes popped. He tucked the collar of his shirt inside and used his two little fingers to make the double pan-pipes of Bacchus's attendant. The photographs were taken. I thanked him, no doubt profusely, and we left.

Harpo Marx *was* the chap in the picture, as I had hoped, though fittingly, not a word of what he said, being who he was, has stayed in my memory.

Matisse

by Edmund Swinglehurst

P ARIS IN THE Fifties was full of artists: GIs who obtained grants from Uncle Sam, Spaniards who had escaped the clutches of Uncle Franco and a polyglot lot who were going to ride on the modern-art bandwagon and had enrolled at the Grande Chaumière, André L'Hote's school, Léger's atelier or the Beaux Arts. I belonged to all of them and my friend Eva posed for Matisse. Did I want to meet him? Yes, please.

He lived in one of those turn-of-the-century apartment blocks with wrought iron lift in Montparnasse and was bedridden, having had a serious operation. He was to die the following year but then he looked very much alive; pale, alert eyes examined me out of a square head covered with bristly white hair. In his right hand he held a bamboo with a pencil stuck in one end. It hovered near the ceiling which was covered with little spirals, like island universes moving into infinity at incalculable speed. What happened when he ran out of ceiling and wall, I wondered. It was not a good opener so I did not say it.

'You're a painter?'

I reeled off a list of ateliers I was attending but he was not impressed. Why should he be?

'The only way to learn is to go out with a pad and pencil and look at nature,' he said. 'Look and draw. Not copy. Draw.'

Almost every painter I knew or had read about said the same thing, including my Spanish friend, Joaquin Peinado, who compared painting to cooking. 'Decide what you are going to cook, work out how to do it and invent the utensils you are going to use.'

I knew Matisse had learned from others like Monet, Cézanne, Bonnard, Signac, and had spent hours copying pictures at the Louvre, but it seemed tactless to mention it.

I looked around the almost empty room in which he lay. Other achievers at the end of their lives surround themselves with evidence of their success but there was nothing like that here. Only the drawings on the ceiling and pinned to the wall. Very simple, very pure – almost childlike.

'Forget everything that people tell you,' he said. 'Clear your mind, then begin.'

It sounded simple enough but it had taken him some 70 years to achieve the kind of drawing that made a significant statement with the barest means.

'Focus on the things you love and find their essence, he said.

He looked at Eva and then at me. 'I want her to come to Nice,' he said. 'But I don't think she'll come.'

Though he must have known that his time was running out he still planned for the future, but he also knew how to accept what could not be. The spirit that inhabits unusual people was still strong in him.

'I was a tiger once,' he said, staring at me, willing me to believe it.

'You still are,' I said and touched his hand briefly. I can still remember the cool, dry feeling of the skin of the hand that painted odalisques and still lifes and decorated the Dominican chapel at Vence.

As we walked down the Boulevard Montparnasse I remembered I had not asked for his autograph or taken his photograph and felt immediately guilty at such a trite idea.

'The other day he told me to take a drawing' Eva said, 'but I did not like to.' He's such a nice old man.'

Henry Miller

by Pauline Podbrey

FIRST HEARD of Henry Miller in South Africa, where I grew up. A friend had smuggled a copy of the forbidden *Tropic of Cancer* through Customs after a holiday abroad and I tried to read it. I was young then and prudish, and I threw it aside in disgust.

Twenty years later in London my colleague Anne Perles invited me to a party given for Henry Miller. Her husband, Alfred Perles, was Miller's friend and confidant, his companion during their days in Clichy and author of the book *My Friend, Henry Miller*.

I arrived full of suppressed excitement. Would I meet an ogre, a Lothario, a sex-crazed seducer? He turned out to be short and balding, with a fleshy lower lip and round, unbecoming spectacles. Only his eyes were remarkable: they were clear and penetrating and he focused intently on whomever he was addressing. His manner was mild and kindly.

A cluster of London literati squatted on the floor at the feet of the Great Man, who was holding forth on art, literature and life. I listened from the outer edges of the circle. Suddenly I pricked up my ears when I heard Miller, replying to a question, say that he did not blame the Italian soldiers who turned tail and ran when confronted by the enemy. 'They were wiser than we were, they loved life, not death,' he told us.

I felt my hackles rise. 'Where would we have been,' I demanded with some heat, 'if our soldiers had refused to fight the Nazis?' 'Well...' he drawled – but Fred Perles did not let him continue. He took him by the arm and led him out into the passageway, from where we heard urgent whispering. When he returned Miller smiled at me kindly. 'I'm sorry,' he said, 'I didn't know you were Jewish.' At this I flared up. 'What difference does it make?' I demanded. 'Surely everyone should feel the same about the Nazis.' Miller tried to placate me but the more he apologised, the angrier I became, to the great consternation of the assembled coterie

The next day Miller phoned and invited me to dinner at Wheeler's. I was intrigued and flattered. It turned out to be one of the most memorable evenings of my life. We talked for about six hours, covering numerous subjects, from women in literature to books and politics. Was I aware of the work of Anaïs Nin, he asked me? When I confessed that I'd never heard of her he advised me to get hold of her books.

I demanded to know why he had refused to sign the anti-Franco petition during the Spanish Civil War when George Orwell had approached him in Paris. 'The issues were so straightforward,' I told him. 'How could you not take sides?' Miller tried to explain to me that he never engaged in political issues or signed petitions of any kind. He, in turn, marvelled at me and my opinions. He'd never met such a political creature, he told me.

We met again during the short time Miller spent in London, and before he left he gave me *To Paint is to Love Again*. Later he sent me the bigger collection of his delightful paintings, *The Angel is My Watermark*. Both of these books are still among my most treasured possessions.

Lord Montgomery

by David Ransom

FIELD MARSHAL LORD Montgomery of Alamein took an interest in a number of boys' schools after the war. Westminster Abbey Choir School, which I attended from 1949 to 1953, was one. His relationship with the school began in 1947 while he was still Chief of the Imperial General Staff. The Dean and Chapter's efforts to re-establish the Choir School quickly after the war were frustrated by the fact that the building

remained in the hands of the War Office. Despite representations at the highest level there seemed little hope of success. Monty had a flat at Westminster, and attended matins at the Abbey. After one such visit, a word in his ear resulted in the building being handed over two weeks later.

So began a long association with the school and its boys. For the Coronation in 1953, his flat having 'gone with the job', Monty and his page lodged with us in Dean's Yard, just behind the Abbey. After one of the final rehearsals, Monty announced that he and his page would pose on the school steps in their full regalia. It was a command rather than an invitation that we should photograph them.

A number of us trooped out dutifully with our Box Brownies. Press photographers were always lurking about in Dean's Yard at that time, and it was no surprise when, the following day, a picture appeared in the *Daily Mirror* of us taking photographs of Monty.

After choir practice that morning I was summoned to the Headmaster's office. There stood Monty and his page. The Headmaster addressed me sternly. 'The Field Marshal would like a word with you,' he said.

'Is that you, boy?' said Monty, pointing to the photograph in the *Daily Mirror* (see previous page). 'Yes sir, it is,' I replied. 'And that's Keith Hewitt and . . . ' I'm not interested in the others,' he interjected. 'Notice anything about the photograph, eh?' I looked at it carefully. 'No sir, I don't. It's rather a good one of . . .' 'SOCKS, boy, SOCKS!' he yelled suddenly. The Headmaster's hand shot to his mouth to stifle a giggle. The page, to whom a number of us had taken a distinct dislike, smirked superciliously.

'You've got one sock up and one sock down,' squeaked a furious Monty. 'You're a disgrace, boy! A disgrace to me and the School. Explain yourself.' I was mortified. 'Gosh, sir,' I said, 'I'm dreadfully sorry. I've lost one of my garters, and . . . I can't explain it, sorry sir.' Monty and the smug-faced page swept out of the room. After more mumbled apologies to the Headmaster, and on the verge of tears, I left the study. I went straight to my copy of the picture and cut off the offending leg. At least my parents would not see my shame when they saw the photograph in my scrapbook, where it remains to this day.

The story might have ended there, but on leaving the Abbey Choir School, I went to St John's School Leatherhead, where Monty was chairman of the governors. An Abbey chorister was a bit of a novelty after the Coronation, and on my first speech day I was called on to the sacred grass of the quad to shake hands with the great man,

'I know you, boy,' he cried, before I could be introduced. 'You're the boy who can't keep his socks up.' He glared at me ferociously and, before I could say anything, added, 'Things don't seem to have improved.' I looked down. No problem there. Even he couldn't see through long trousers. Shoes looked OK. 'Your JACKET,' he shrieked. 'It's got a button missing!'

Laurence Olivier

by John Wells

THE LATE SIR Laurence Olivier exercised an eerie fascination over me from the first time I ever saw him act in the film version of *Hamlet*. It was something to do with the way he arranged his face before he spoke, and then pushed the familiar English language about into weird shapes, rather in the way Gerald Scarfe distorts the human face. It was still recognisable as English, but the pleasure was not so much in listening to the meaning as to the funny cadences, the unexpected swoops, mutters and yelps. It was a style that achieved its fullest flowering in his *Richard III*, where the distortions in the language were echoed by the cartoon figure on the screen, the hump, the nose and the funny walk. I first saw him in the flesh, without really meeting him, in Sean Kenny's office in Greek Street some time in 1964, when he came in to talk about the set for a play Sean was designing. Sean was a small, tough, broad-shouldered Irishman, who could lift a car onto the pavement if he didn't like the way it was parked and frequently hit people, and I was alarmed when Sir Laurence laid a languid arm round his shoulders, rolled his eyes and said, 'Hello, Shawnie Baby!' Sean didn't hit him, but I was surprised how concerned Olivier was about timing and delivery, even off stage. I am not sure whether that mystery was solved about five years after that, when I met him. I had translated *Danton's Death* for the National Theatre. The play was directed by Jonathan Miller, and Christopher Plummer was playing Danton. Shortly before the dress rehearsal there was some disagreement or other. Christopher Plummer was brooding in his dressing room, and Olivier, the director of the National Theatre, came down to the theatre to smooth things over. Jonathan Miller had encouraged the designers to eschew the obvious, and apart from some glass cases containing dresses, the only scenery consisted of two plaster figures accurately modelled on the male anatomy – with the skin or muscles peeled back here and there to demonstrate the working parts – standing left and right on either side of the forestage. Both were, I think, modelled from life, one with ampler external organs than the other. It was to this one that Sir Laurence seemed drawn, and we ambled across the stage to examine it. After a while he asked Jonathan in the familiar cracked articulation: 'Tell me, Jon-ath-an, sum-

thing I have nevah un–der–stood: How does the *bludd* get into the *pee-nis* to create an *e-rec-shun*?' Jonathan fluttered his hands and explained with his characteristic hurried hesitancy that, 'it wasn't so much the blood getting into the penis, it was more a kind of brake operation that prevented it from getting out.' Sir Lawrence pondered this in silence for a moment or two, and then said with the familiar upward inflection, *'Ejaculatio praecox . . . The story of my life!'*

George Orwell

by Stella Judt

I T MUST HAVE been around the early 1930s that the gentleman char came into my mother's life. I helped her in the house after school, as had my older sisters, but they were now out at work. How she coped, in that old, cold, inconvenient, no-amenities house was truly amazing. We were a family of ten, with huge appetites, and we frequently brought hungry friends home for meals. My mother could stretch a meal quite miraculously. We lived in Limehouse, close to the docks (the area now featured in the TV soap *East Enders*).

One day a friend who lived near Whitechapel's Rowton House, a hostel for the homeless, brought 'Laurel' to our house. His real name was not known; 'Laurel' was the label attached to him by the East Enders with whom he came into contact. He was prepared to clean our house for the going rate of half a crown (12½ pence) a day, plus a midday meal. The money just about covered the cost of a bed at Rowton House, and possibly some cigarettes.

I came home early one afternoon and there he was. The tall, slim, narrow-faced 'charman' bore a resemblance to the Laurel of the much-loved comedy partnership Laurel and Hardy.

The man spoke to me. It was not what he said that startled me, it was the way he said it. His speech was what we at that time called Oxford English, cultured, correct, plum-in-the-mouth BBC English. I was too young then to hide my surprise at his posh accent. He smiled gently, bowed slightly, and then further astonished me by kissing my mother's hand and saying, 'Goodbye, queen of the kitchen'. Turning to me he added, 'Your mother is a fine lady and a splendid cook'.

My mother was consumed with pity for the poor man. She told me that he had scrubbed all the floors, cleaned the twin outside lavatories and polished the blacklead cooker to a mirror finish. 'That well-bred gentleman worked so hard I had to make him stop for a rest.'

Then, quite suddenly, Laurel vanished. He was seen no more in our part of the East End. He was just another of the anonymous men who overnighted at the doss house.

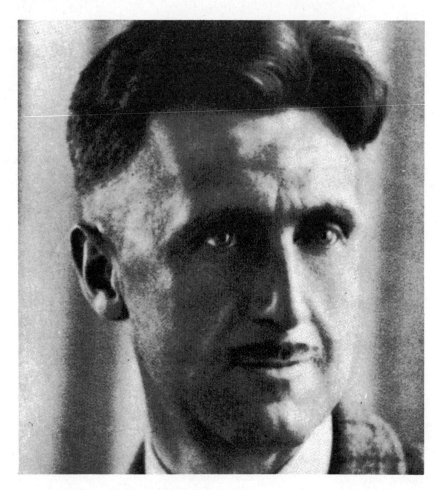

After the last war, I came upon a book written by George Orwell. In it was a photograph of the author, taken when younger. The man was Eric Blair, and I recognised him. He was my mother's Laurel; it must have been during his period of tramping around London, doing any work that came his way, that he did his East End charring.

George Orwell was reputed to have said that the women he admired most were the hardworking, uncomplaining mothers of at least eight children. I like to think that he included my mother in this. She certainly fitted the description.

Dorothy Parker

by Phoebe Winch

N THE EARLY 1950s I was a journalist, and during a visit to New York, thought I'd try and interview Dorothy Parker whom I'd long admired, not just for her wit, but also for her less well-known short stories. I was convinced an article about the reclusive Queen of the Algonquin set would be snapped up by any editor.

I finally found her in a small residential hotel in a slightly seedy, but genteel, district of Manhattan. The doorman was attentive: he was used to the demands of small dogs and old ladies. The lift was slow and the corridors were dark.

'We all live here,' said Dorothy Parker as she opened the door, 'until we are carried out.'

Her dog, a poodle, yapped and jumped about. 'He thinks he is a very large watch- dog,' she said, giving him some biscuits to keep him quiet and pouring herself a large whisky. She was very small, perhaps in her late fifties, and her black hair was shingled in the 20s style. She was wearing a slightly 'bohemian' blouse covered in multi-coloured cross-stitching.

Her eyes were large and dark, and kept dimming behind a veil of watery sadness, then a few moments later would appear once more bright and alive. Her voice, hoarse and quiet, also disappeared into depths of unhappiness, until she forced it out a little louder in staccato jerks.

'Was I funny once? I don't remember. I don't think I ever intended to be funny. It all seems such a long time ago. Do people really still quote me? I can hardly believe it. Do you really mean that? How wonderful!'

She seemed intensely sad, and to plead for encouragement. But, determined not to be maudlin, she pulled herself sharply together.

'What did I do after the 20s? I went to Hollywood. It was terrible. I hated every moment I was there. I wrote film scripts, such bad film scripts, I can't even remember their names. It is a hateful place.

'Then I married, and we bought a farm as a reaction against Hollywood life. But farming is hateful too, and farmers are such miserable people, never happy whatever the weather. Our farm didn't make any money, of course, so we had

to go back to Hollywood for a few months each year to make enough money to keep on farming.

'Then I got divorced, and went to Mexico. Beautiful, colourful and exciting, at first. But it is such a sad place. You suddenly notice the poverty, and I was ashamed of my rich, drunk ex-compatriots who rode on the shoulders of the poor. So Mexico became too sad, and I came to New York.

'Now I wake up every morning, ready to kiss the pavements of this city, not because it is New York, but because it isn't Hollywood.

'How can I be funny? There isn't anything to be funny about. The world is not a funny place. I am writing plays with Arnaud d'Usseau. Our last one, *Ladies of the Corridor,* was a serious play, but it lost money because there were seven changes of scene. I must make some money, but this new play we are doing won't run for long either. It is very serious, about a homosexual, but music and dancing girls keep creeping in, which will put up the cost, won't it? Oh dear.

'Goodbye. Must you be going? Thank you so much for coming to see me. I find it hard to believe that anyone will be interested in me.'

Rachmaninoff

by Joseph Cooper

THE NAME RACHMANINOFF was familiar to me from the age of four. My mother, an excellent amateur pianist, would on request thunder out Rachmaninoff's famous *Prelude in C sharp minor.* I used to sit on a cushion under our Steinway grand, because the climax sounded even louder there. How I adored that piece.

I didn't know the composer was a great pianist until I was thirteen and became a music scholar at Clifton College under William McKie (later Sir William, organist of Westminster Abbey). We went to various celebrity concerts at the Colston Hall, Bristol, but the greatest occasion for me was a recital by Rachmaninoff. He came onto the platform, gaunt and unsmiling, hardly

acknowledging the applause, and started to play. The hall filled with brilliant and colourful sounds I never dreamt a piano could make, and the slower melodies – especially in Chopin – seemed to take on the quality of the human voice: Rachmaninoff could make a piano sing! For an encore he played the *C sharp minor Prelude*. As I left the hall, I was euphoric. Could I ever recapture some of the great man's tone-colouring in my own playing? Rachmaninoff became my musical hero and I longed to meet him, even for a brief second.

The chance came in 1938 at the Savage Club in London, where he was to be the guest of his friend and compatriot, Benno Moiseiwitsch. I took along my copy of the *3rd Piano Concerto*, hoping to have it autographed. At the end of dinner I followed the two great pianists out of the dining room, but to my horror I realised they were making for the loo! Determined not to miss my chance, I waited at the door. I could hear them talking in English, which was encouraging. As they re-appeared I held out the copy and said, 'Would you please, Mr Rachmaninoff?' 'Yes, of course,' he replied and, in his spidery writing, he signed my copy of the Concerto. We shook hands.

Over half a century later the magical moment of meeting Rachmaninoff lives with me still.

Lord Reith
by Mike Leburn

THE OCCASION WAS the opening of a new factory in East Africa in the late fifties. This had been developed by the Commonwealth Development Corporation of which, at that time, Lord Reith was Chairman. He was not personally opening the factory. This was being done by the Governor of the Territory.

As I was in charge of the opening arrangements I met him at the airport where he was arriving by private plane. How he got into that little aircraft, I don't know, but he surely had an awful job getting out, this huge gaunt figure with a formidable face – a face almost of doom and menace with its large hooked nose, downturned mouth, and above all its sunken scar high on his left cheek. I was very nervous having heard much of his reputation of management by fear. Looking at him one could imagine him preaching Hellfire and Brimstone from a Presbyterian pulpit for an hour or two on a Sunday morning in Scotland.

The journey from the airport to the Company guest house where he was staying was largely conducted in silence except for the occasional groan presumably indicating pain in his cramped limbs. On arrival he insisted on examining every aspect of the guest house. The bedroom first. 'I presume that bed is at least seven foot long,' he said. 'You must surely have been informed that I must have a special bed.'

'Well yes, Sir,' I replied. 'But I was totally unable to get one in this rather underdeveloped country so I put in a double bed hoping that it would be satisfactory if you slept diagonally across it.'

'Are you sure you have got the geometry of this correct?' he grudgingly growled.

The bathroom next. 'That mirror above the basin, it's been set up for a dwarf. I can't possibly shave if I can't see my face. Get it hung another two feet higher immediately.'

The sitting room next. Much to my relief at this point the wife of one of the directors appeared – a well-appointed, nearly middle-aged female of considerable charm. The atmosphere changed immediately.

His Lordship positively enthused over her and as the sun was down ordered me to produce drinks for us all. She had whisky and I said to him I had fresh orange or fresh lime or tonic water. 'What do mean?' he said. 'I'll have whisky with a little water.' I was a little taken aback as I had been informed he was tee-total. So I poured him a little whisky, gave it to him and proffered the water jug. 'What do you call this?' he said. 'Give me a proper whisky.'

An hour later the best part of the bottle had gone. And so we left him to have his shower as later there was a reception in the club for him to meet the staff. His parting shot to me was: 'When meeting the staff I must have a glass of orange juice in my hand. I will not be seen in public drinking alcohol.' A neat little piece of hypocrisy if ever there was one.

The next morning when the factory opening was about halfway through I decided to go to the club to see if the celebratory lunch arrangements were in order. I was looking at name place cards on the top table and was infuriated to see that they had all been altered. Who on earth had done that? Suddenly I knew. At the back of the dining room, astonishingly, there emerged from the clearly marked ladies' lavatory door this gaunt frightening figure.

'Leburn!' he roared. 'Do you realise there is only one towel in the ladies lavatory?'

I was speechless. Later my thought was, only, if only, there had been a lady in the lavatory.

Bertrand Russell

by Stephen Parkinson

I N SEPTEMBER 1948, as a reporter on what we were proud to call the *Manchester Guardian*, I was on holiday in Trondheim, Norway, with a local journalist, Eystein Dohl. Such was the prestige of the *Guardian* that Eystein interviewed me for his paper (he was paid on lineage!), and as a result the students' union at the university invited me to a lecture by Bertrand Russell.

For two days we had endured high winds and driving rain. On the morning of Russell's arrival we were surprised by the number of ambulances racing through the town. Someone told us that in the wind a seaplane had crashed into the fjord drowning 19 people. Also, a famous British philosopher was on board.

After that Eystein and I moved faster than the wind. Russell had been taken to an hotel where the manager would not let us see him. Fortunately the president of the students' union was about to visit him and he took us in with him.

We learned that Russell had sat at the rear of the plane so that he could smoke his pipe. Those in front could not escape when the plane nose-dived into the water but someone pushed Russell through a window and he swam around in the icy fjord for two or three minutes before being picked up.

So there he was sitting up in bed, reading a thriller and smoking a pipe. He looked extraordinarily elfish and apologised for being in bed, due, he said, to having been up at an 'unchristian' hour to catch the plane.

His nonchalance was amazing for a man of seventy-six after such a terrifying experience but it seemed to me that he was enjoying the limelight and the admiration of everyone around him.

'I always wondered what I would say in such a situation,' he said. 'I imagined I would say something extreme like 'damnation!' but, you know, all I said was 'well, well'. Nobody asked me if I could swim. They just pushed me unceremoniously out of a window.'

Quaking at the effrontery of such a question, I asked, '*Can* you swim?'

'Of course I can,' he replied indignantly. 'But it is a little difficult in one's overcoat. Also I was trying to hang on to my attaché case but in the end I had to let it go. Now I have no papers but so far no-one seems to doubt that I am me.'

Nor did they. Later he gave his lecture on *Ideologies and Common Sense*. Whatever his merits as a philosopher the students thought he was a great and brave man.

As for me my main anxiety was how to get the story to Manchester out of my £35 allowance. There were severe limits on money for foreign travel in those days but my Norwegian friends rallied round and my reward came later when I bought a *Manchester Guardian* in Stockholm and saw my scoop displayed prominently on the front page.

Margaret Rutherford

by John Hindle

A
FTER THE LAST 1956 Olympic race had been run and the spectators scurried back to their many nations, Melbourne sweated through long months of cloudless summer and congratulated itself on becoming 'cosmopolitan'.

During that December my father, who did not wish to be cosmopolitan, took me to two British films, *Blithe Spirit* and *The Happiest Days of Your Life*. My father admired several British actresses, but he adored Margaret Rutherford. He even bought tickets for the stage production of *The Happiest Days* at the Princess Theatre, with Miss Rutherford as Miss Whitchurch.

Dad counted the days until the performance. I was considerably less excited and simply went about my business, which was usually conducted at the Middle Brighton sea baths. I trained there at six o'clock each morning, then devoted myself to suntanned hedonism until sunset. I'm sure that my father would have joined me had he known that my early-morning swims would bring me into contact with his idol.

In those days the baths were home to many eccentrics. Our Icebergers, for instance, whooped and spluttered at the deep end; a young seminarian counted grains of sand on the beach each morning; and old Mr Telford, the advertising man, liked to hang by his toes from the diving board and sway in the breeze, like a giant albino fruit bat, until metatarsal fatigue caused him to drop gracelessly into the sea.

But nobody except Miss Rutherford walked to the baths wearing an old woollen swim-suit, a cotton dressing-gown, a yellow bathing cap, and strange, English foot-wear called 'plimsolls'.

I was the first person Miss Rutherford spoke to at the baths: 'Young man! Would you be kind enough to ensure that I don't drown?' I watched as she trudged, safely, across the 55-yard width of the baths, and helped her as she climbed the steps to the safety of the boardwalk. Her chins, which seemed to have lives of their own, wobbled wetly as she sucked the morning air and asked me a personal question: 'Are you regular?'

My mother was the last person who had asked me that, when I was nine. I didn't know where to look.

'Are you regular, boy?' she persisted. 'Do you come here each morning?' Ahhh, relief! I told her that I was very regular indeed.

'Then you may save my life six mornings a week,' she said. Dripping and wheezing, Miss Rutherford headed for the exit, but was stopped by Old Tim, the baths' manager, who asked her a question: 'Breakfast?'

'That would be lovely,' she said, and she joined us most mornings during her Melbourne season. We all thought she was wonderful. Miss Rutherford insisted that I bring my father backstage after *The Happiest Days*. She duchessed him mercilessly, and he loved it.

Haile Selassie I
by Richard Snailham

WE HAD JUST completed the first descent of the Ethiopian section of the Blue Nile in inflatable dinghies and the Emperor Haile Selassie, for whose Wild Life Department we had done the journey, invited the whole 65 of us to one of his palaces in Addis Ababa.

It was thought appropriate that we should give our host a present, and a sounding of his advisers revealed that he was fond of Chihuahua dogs. So

'Betteena of Benrue' was purchased in Shropshire, renamed Lulette to match Lulu, a Chihuahua he already had, and flown out.

We all assembled at the Jubilee Palace and were ushered forward in a long line. The form was to enter the audience chamber, stop, bow, proceed halfway towards the imperial presence, stop and bow again, and then march on to just in front of the little man at a point whence it was possible to shake hands easily without stretching unnaturally or looming intimidatingly (most of us, including Blashford-Snell, our leader, were over 6ft tall).

The last chap in the line bore Lulette on a velvet cushion and presented her. The Emperor smiled – a rare thing – picked her up, stroked her and set her down on the ground, whereupon Lulette walked to the side of the throne, cocked a leg and peed. The Emperor smiled again, a little less warmly, and said, 'It shows she is at home.'

In fact, I met him twice. He came to take a parade at the Royal Military Academy Sandhurst where one of his many grandsons, David Makonnen, was a cadet and where I was a senior lecturer. As I had visited Ethiopia several times I was in the luncheon party and was afterwards ushered forward for a few words. I told the Emperor that David was doing well at his German. There was a long pause and then with great solemnity he opined, 'It is important to learn the languages of other peoples.' Great men get by on such banalities.

George Bernard Shaw

by Christine Porteus

MET HIM twice, both times getting the same reaction – blue eyes blazing, stick held high and something being shouted. I am sure I represented the type of human being he loathed – namely a child. We lived in the village next to Ayot St Lawrence in those far off days when parents took their offspring for longish walks. Looking back I suspect this was a method of tiring out healthy children. Shaw's village was very small, a straggle of cottages

and middle-sized houses, a pseudo-classical temple and a ruined church. Not much else. A 17th-century cottage doubled as the post office, presided over by Gysbella Lyte who, like Shaw, had something of a reputation. Shaw's house stood darkly at a corner. In fact it was called 'Shaw's Corner'.

On my first meeting with the old man I was peering through his gate hoping to catch sight of him. I did. He appeared in the gloom of his drive waving his stick, eyebrows electrically alert, eyes flashing, shouting at me – 'Get away from my gate, urchin'. The aura of temper hanging around this tall, skinny, knickerbockered man was enough to send any child running. I ran.

Our second meeting, perhaps a year later, took place in the dark lane leading to 'Shaw's Corner'. He had walked to the post office, no doubt to post more of his famous cards and was wending his way slowly back to his house. I was skipping along in the opposite direction. I remember he stood still at the sight of a child having the audacity to be in his lane. Up flew the walking stick yet again, eyebrows unfurled, blue eyes hard as ice with annoyance froze me and an acid, high-pitched squeak issued forth. I was terrified and ran back down the lane to hide until he had passed.

When Shaw died his body was carried to Mr Blow, the undertaker in our village, and many important people came to view the great man. I was told that Shaw had died with his mouth open as if in speech – about to shout at somebody I expect! A small block of wood was hidden beneath his beard to wedge shut his mouth. An over-eager viewer knocked the bier, the wedge flew out and Shaw's mouth fell open. Consternation from the body-watchers. Was the old man still alive and about to utter yet again?

Tom Stoppard

by David Stafford

IN THE MID 1960s, when being tired and emotional meant your name was George Brown, I shared a mansion flat with friends on the wrong side of Vincent Square. Gently perfumed with boiled cabbage and old feet, the building sheltered a motley lot of dipsomaniacs, bisexuals, ex-Tory ministers, and trench coats from the MI6 office round the corner on Vauxhall Bridge Road. Going to and from work we would furtively eye each other in the corridors, and at weekends would even risk a nod when lifting in the milk that was still, in those far off days, delivered by a cheery milkman who doffed his cap and said 'Good morning, sir'.

One of the denizens of this Edwardian sepulchre was a lean young man, barely older than myself, who scurried in and out at odd hours dressed in a black velvet jacket and trousers that aged noticeably over the months. Pale and intense, with raven hair that curled wildly around his pallid features, he was obviously drawn by some unseen force that propelled him along the corridors

like the March Hare. Sometimes he would be seen with a small child, or a woman, or both. The three lived directly above us, and often we would hear the child crying. Rumour had it that he was artistic.

At this time, as a noviciate in the Foreign Office, I kept gentleman's hours, which meant that crises never happened before ten o'clock and a full reading of *The Times*. So everyone else had left for work when there was a knock at the door and I opened it to find the black velvet suit. Its occupant smiled, apologised for the intrusion, and asked if we might do him a favour. He had, he explained, noted that we were out during the daytime. As a writer whose concentration was distracted by a crying infant, could he possibly use our kitchen table to write on during the day, when everyone was out? I should explain that the table was a bit of a sore point. For some mystical reason one of my flatmates, an expert on medieval theology, had ordered one that was eight feet square. The result was no floor space and a table that could seat the twelve disciples. It definitely needed more using. So to get rid of the eccentric scribbler I said yes. I didn't even bother with his name.

For the next few months I saw nothing of him. The only reminder of his existence was the coffee cup he always left unwashed in the sink and the unending litter of crumpled paper he threw into the wastepaper basket. Once I inspected it, only to find that every sheet was blank. This confirmed me in my pin-striped view that he was a wastrel, and I went about my own business of saving the world with an increased sense of purpose.

Then, one evening, he called to say he had completed his manuscript. 'Manuscript?' I echoed, not quite believing my ears and thinking of the forests he'd massacred in our kitchen. 'Oh, yes,' he smiled, 'I've been writing a play.' He must have seen the disbelief on my face. 'It's about a couple of characters from Shakespeare,' he explained, 'what happens behind the scenes.' Deranged, I thought, but felt compelled to be polite. 'Oh, who?' I asked. 'Rosencrantz and Guildenstern,' he replied, 'from Hamlet'. I looked at the decayed velvet suit and his big black eyes staring at me from his mop of hair. Then I knew he was crazy.

Jacques Tati

by Jonathan Abbott

I N THE EARLY Sixties, I was involved in starting an advertising agency, which, at that time, hadn't become such a commonplace event. To our surprise, we were appointed by one of the major high street banks. My particular responsibility was writing and producing film commercials, and, as our new client had lagged behind in this sector, I was anxious to impress both him and the advertising industry at large by suggesting that Jacques Tati be invited to make one for us. The script I had concocted for the allegedly more caring bank made its point via Tati's well-known antipathy to automation with a neat little common-man-versus-the-computer plot.

My idea was accepted and I was despatched to Paris to engage the great man, who suggested a number of improvements to the basic idea. He then took me into a cutting-room and showed me a rough version of his forthcoming film, *Traffic*, as he was concerned about a sequence at a petrol station and a joke about a motorist – overloaded with free gifts. He asked me how this could be improved and, keen to respond to the maestro, I said it might be funnier if the gift was more incongruous, say a small bust of Beethoven. Tati fixed me with a cold look and we returned to his office to discuss his fee for the commercial and the logistics of filming it.

As he was about to leave, he suddenly asked 'What about casting?'. This came as a nasty shock as my idea depended on the use of his Monsieur Hulot character, complete with hat, pipe, Burberry and umbrella (the fee I had agreed also reflected this, I felt). Tati was adamant. M. Hulot wasn't on the menu. It would not be difficult to find an English actor he could bend to his will. For the rest of the participants, he always relied on real people. The employees of the bank would be ideal.

I returned to London dreading the next meeting with the client. I reported that it was all systems go: Tati was crazy about the idea, but there was a snag – he wouldn't actually figure in the commercial, just direct it. I shut my eyes and waited for blows to rain down on me. 'Thank goodness for that,' I heard the client say. 'We didn't like to say that we felt M. Hulot was a little old for our target audience.'

A branch of the bank was chosen for its charm and negotiations were completed for its staff to come in over the weekend to appear in the film. Tati asked to be booked into a simple little pub, whose name he could never pronounce, which turned out to be the Connaught. Shortly after filming started, a worried assistant director told me that Tati would like a word. 'Do you 'ave a black book?' asked the maestro. 'You know, phone numbers of actresses, models, mistresses, etcetera?' I spent the rest of the day on the telephone trying to rustle up talent. The film turned out better than I expected and Tati disappeared from my life. Shortly afterwards, I received two tickets for the premiere of *Traffic*. In the middle of the film was quite a funny scene at a petrol station with a motorist's glove compartment crammed with little busts of Beethoven.

Kenneth Tynan

by Robin Rook

WE WENT TO the first Edinburgh Festival from Oxford together. There were four of us, a motley crew: Ken, the thinking man's Aguecheek; Lindsay Anderson, a diminutive Pantaloon; myself, the boring juvenile lead; and Byng, our minder, a natural for the front row of any rugby scrum.

Ken had fixed everything and made only one mistake, the hotel: well-sited but temperance and with rules to match. We lasted three days: first day, no problem; second, locked out with Byng climbing the Regency portico and entering through an Australian girl's window; third, caught playing strip-poker with said girl. Ken's visit nearly ended prematurely too, when he formed an instant infatuation (as was his wont) for the soprano playing Susanna in the Glyndebourne production of *Figaro*. After the performance, armed with a huge bouquet, he talked his way into her dressing room. The snag was that she was Turkish. As he was making his presentation he sensed a malign presence behind him and, glancing over his shoulder, saw the most *enormous* janissary standing by the door.

My reward for becoming his friend was to be given the lead in Byron's *Manfred* but after disconcertingly few rehearsals (about two?) he decided that either it was unactable or that I could not act it; uncharacteristically he did not say which – at least not to me. To meet his commitment to the Experimental Theatre Club, he cobbled together a brilliant pastiche of the Hamlet/Ophelia relationship, which he called *A Toy in Blood*. I played Hamlet in a white shirt with red pyjama bottoms, tactfully sewn up the front by my landlady. Army experience came in handy when I had to pursue Claudius in a blackout which culminated with 'Dead for a ducat, dead' – *bang!* I fired a revolver straight at the audience.

My great scene was anticipated one night when the two of us were eating at the Taj Mahal in the Turl after the pubs had shut and a drunken hearty lurched over to our table to boast in none too friendly a tone that he was meeting Cyril Connolly next night and had we any message for him? 'Yes', said Ken, 'give him our regards and say, "In thy *Horizons* be all our sins remembered".'

When I came to play the nunnery scene, Ken had me in bed with a silent whore whom Hamlet, now a misogynist, taunts, 'You jig, you amble, and you lisp, and nickname God's creatures, and make your wantonness your ignorance . . . ' Telephone rings, Hamlet answers, Ophelia says, 'My honour'd lord . . . ' Hamlet cuts her short with, 'To a nunnery, go; and quickly too. Farewell.' He rings off. Ophelia dabs at the telephone with her finger, 'O heavenly powers, restore him!'

Ken's burlesque ended with the appearance of two American journalists at Ophelia's burial. One asks 'Whose grave's this?' and on being told, 'One that was a woman, sir; but, rest her soul, she's dead,' says dismissively, 'Lay her i' th' earth,' as his black companion takes a photograph, firing his flash-gun like an echo of her father's earlier death. Ken was an iconoclast even then.

Roger Vadim
by Viola von Harrach

THE WHITE SANDY beach was littered with debris, palm fronds, pieces of coral, tattered lengths of rope, a myriad of strange fish which lay like dull jewels at the water's edge along with other dead and dying sea creatures: the leftovers flagrantly scattered after the hurricane had supped and blown itself out during the night. It was an extraordinary sight.

Aged sixteen, I was at that unequal stage that hovers somewhat precariously between the woman, flaunting my Way In bikini, and the gauche, rather volatile adolescent. It was the mid-60s. My father, a barrister, was working on a brief in the Bahamas and we were with him on holiday.

After the relentless noise of the hurricane, the morning after – the morning I met Roger Vadim – was uneasily quiet, the sun limpid and, because it was still early, the long arm of the beach deserted. The sand, usually virginal and pallid, looked that morning as if it had been monstrously violated. Strewn across it in careless abandon was a fascinating array of deep-sea creatures, some seemingly

gnawed and spat out in what can only be described as the worst possible taste, others regurgitated along with torn scales and fins and innards.

The jellyfish appeared to be the only survivor. A spectacular sight, brightly coloured in shades of green, purple and blue, it was obviously fighting for life. Knowing that as the sun's heat grew stronger, the jellyfish would die, I rushed back to our apartment, which was only a few hundred yards from the beach, and grabbed the first things that came to hand – a pink plastic dustbin with a lid, and a mop. Using the mop and the lid I was struggling to slide the jellyfish into the bin when a voice behind me said, 'What are you doing that for? Can I be of assistance?'

I explained that the deep sea aquarium further along the coast had asked people to bring in unusual sea creatures, and that the jellyfish had a chance of survival, if I could get it there.

Even with two of us, it took some time to get the jellyfish into the bin, edging it with the mop as carefully as we could so as not to damage it. It was a slightly farcical, incongruous situation, what with the jellyfish lashing about and us jumping out of the way to avoid getting stung. Intent on our task, we really only exchanged pleasantries – where I was staying, where he was staying, the usual trivialities. Having succeeded, he then filled the lid with sea-water and poured it purposefully over the hapless creature. The lid was put firmly on the bin and we carried it between us back to the apartment.

'By the way, my name is Roger, Roger Vadim,' he said. There was an awkward silence. He probably expected me to react, but I didn't. I'm ashamed to admit that I had no idea who Roger Vadim was. 'Susan Marsh,' I said. We shook hands rather formally. Then hesitantly, almost as an afterthought, he suggested that I meet him for a drink at his hotel that evening. We fixed a time, and that was it. He walked off back along the beach and I went to ask my father to drive the dustbin full of jellyfish to the aquarium.

There is a sting to this tale. When I related this episode to my father, he was furious that I had accepted an invitation from a stranger and 'one with such a reputation'. Worse still, later that day I found I was covered in small spots and German Measles was diagnosed. I suppose I should have phoned his hotel and explained, but at sixteen the thought was too embarrassing. So I never got to meet Roger Vadim again.

Evelyn Waugh

by Hugh Burnett

EVELYN WAUGH WAS at his eccentric best in 1953 when we arrived to record an interview for Far Eastern listeners at Pier's Court in Stinchcombe, known to friends as 'Stinkers', its brass plate announcing 'No Admittance on Business'. As the recording cable was run in to the house he expressed great concern that his wife's cows, chewing the cud in a field a hundred yards away, should not be electrocuted by accident. After some confusion the interview began. He chose to sit behind his desk in the library, wearing a grey suit, waistcoat, watch-chain and a Brigade of Guards tie. 'My original ambition was to become a painter and after that a carpenter,' he declared. 'But I found that I was too lazy to acquire very much facility in either of these crafts, while my whole education had gone to make me literary.'

Drink had been his main interest at university. 'I took a bad Third.' All music was painful to him, with the possible exception of plainchant. Decent architecture ceased about the time he was born.

This visit preceded publication of *The Ordeal of Gilbert Pinfold*, a name borrowed from an earlier owner of Pier's Court. Pinfold was harassed by the voice of a BBC interviewer. So why did Waugh agree in 1960 to go on television in *Face to Face*? He requested a ridiculously large fee and a contract was devised including every conceivable right. He accepted. Had he agreed the original offer the total would have been greatly increased by repeat fees.

I went with Felix Topolski for lunch to Combe Florey, near Taunton, a house without a television set and a radio only in the servants' quarters. He pretended to be surprised that we had not arrived, as gentlemen normally did, by train. Over lunch he asked what would be required of him. 'Will the studio be very hot? Would I need to wear my tropical clothes?' I assured him that the black drapes of the set would keep him cool. 'You mean I'll be given one to wear?' When the time came for Topolski to start sketching Waugh was aghast. 'But where's your easel, Mr Topolski? What! You don't use an easel?' As Felix sketched Waugh discussed, among many things, buggery on Mount Athos. Then it was time for afternoon tea. As we got up I admired the chandelier. 'That's not a chandelier – that's a gasolier! Are you interested in gasoliers?' and off I was taken to admire the gasoliers. We arrived in the dining-room where a large tureen of green-tufted strawberries was waiting. Too late I saw the problem. Put the strawberries on the plate, add the cream, take the spoon – and you were trapped with the strawberry tufts. My attempt to spear one shot it under the sideboard. That was the BBC disgraced. Topolski, seeing what had happened, did the socially unthinkable – dipped a strawberry into the cream with his fingers. 'Ah, Mr Topolski,' Waugh observed helpfully, 'you need a spoon.'

When he arrived at Lime Grove it became clear that his illness had not completely evaporated. 'Where's the hidden microphone?' he enquired. His eyes settled on the wire of the electric clock. 'Ah yes. I see.' When John Freeman arrived I introduced them. Waugh stepped back horrified. 'The name is Waugh – not Wuff!' he protested. 'But I called you Mr Waugh,' Freeman smiled. 'No, no, I distinctly heard you say "Wuff",' continued the great writer, lighting a cigar. I read later that he had checked for any defamatory information about his interviewer in case he needed it for defence or offence.

When asked why he was appearing on television he replied: 'Poverty. We are both being hired to talk in this deliriously happy way.' Freeman challenged him on this pose of poverty. Waugh replied: 'Never saved a penny. And of course no honest man has been able to save any money in the last 20 years.' His worst fault was irritability. With? 'Absolutely everything. Inanimate objects and people, animals, anything.'

The game continued after the filming. A postcard, addressed to 'The Director General of *Face to Face*' said he had found a cigar cutter in his pocket which was not his. Was it mine? I replied that I was not missing a cigar cutter. Another card arrived after the film was transmitted. 'Thank you for your letter. I did not see the exhibition but somebody who did remarked that it seemed to end abruptly. I assure you I don't care. EW, SS Peter & Paul 1960.' The transmission had indeed ended abruptly. John Freeman had asked as a closing question whether, looking back on the mental breakdown, he could see a conflict between the way he had been brought up and the lifestyle he had chosen to live. 'Oh, I know what you're getting at. That ass Priestley said that in an article . . . Poor old Priestley thought that.' BBC lawyers decided the reference might take us all into court, so it was chopped off. A pity because Priestley v Waugh on whether Priestley was an ass would have been worth every penny of a legal action.

Wavell

by Mervyn Horder

ACTUALLY IT WAS twice. The first time was in 1943 while he was C-in-C India, when one morning in GHQ Delhi I was told by Peter Fleming, who worked in the same room as I did, that Wavell wanted to see me. Instant cashiering perhaps? But that didn't seem likely as I was in the RAF not the army. Fleming took me along the corridor and we found the Field Marshal in shorts standing at a high desk in his room, surrounded by the galley proofs of his verse anthology *Other Men's Flowers*. Without preamble he asked me who the 'Daniel George' might be who had peppered these proofs with cross-references, notes, suggestions and other editorialities. Was he any good? I told him D G was Jonathan Cape's editorial advisor. Cape had found him working as a humble clerk in Ewart's Geysers in the Euston Road.

'*Geysers?*' His tone was exactly that of Lady Bracknell with the handbag. I gave him what reassurance I could, not so much from my own knowledge of D G as from my respect for Cape, who had that strange entrepreneur's flair for paying the right person the right sum for the right advice and, I knew, would not make a mistake over choosing an editor for such a job. Wavell seemed satisfied, but wouldn't allow me to correct his proofs in any way, as I offered to do. He was clearly going to enjoy that job by himself. The second confrontation was in March 1946, with Wavell now Viscount Wavell of Cyrenaica and Winchester, His Majesty's Viceroy and Governor-General of India. I was stopping over in Delhi on the way home from a stint in Tokyo during the first six months of the American occupation. I was bidden to a large lunch, some twenty outside guests, in Viceregal Lodge. These affairs were a torment for a man of Wavell's reserved temperament. Protocol demanded that after lunch each guest be brought up by an ADC to sit alone with the Viceroy on a sofa for five minutes. Protocol didn't demand, but Lady Wavell did, that she sit on a nearby facing sofa to support him through these distasteful encounters. When I got to the sofa, a wintry smile of welcome replaced the viceregal frown for a moment, but there was no nonsense about viceroyalty initiating any subject of conversation. There was no conversation. (I thought it too corny to refer to the fact that we were both Winchester college men.) Still no conversation. I then

had an inspiration: remembering the prominence he had given in *Other Men's Flowers* to Belloc's verse, and something else I had heard, I kicked off in a dreamy sort of way:

> *The chief defect of Henry King*
> *Was chewing little bits of string . . .*

After the merest hint of a pause, the Viceroy of India chimed in with the rest

> *At last he swallowed one which tied*
> *Itself in nasty knots inside . . .*

And we were well away. We did the last line in unison. Since the firm I worked for in peace time, Duckworth, published in those days all Belloc's poetry, I was able to give him a good deal of curious information about Belloc and his publishing contracts. I was asked to stay behind after the other guests had gone, given free use of the viceregal swimming pool and so on.

Indians had a fellow feeling for Wavell – old, wise and adding to the oriental his own brand of British inscrutability. He was one of those men, like A E Housman (and indeed like the present author), who given the chance would pass the whole of their lives in unbroken silence. I am pleased that he twice broke it to me.

H G Wells

by Vincent Brome

THE HOUSE WAS No 13 Hanover Terrace, deliberately chosen to taunt the superstitious. The maid showed me to the 'sun-trap', a room at the top of the house which concentrated available sunshine. As I entered I could hear Mozart playing and there, nodding asleep in front of the gramophone, was the man who had inspired my life – and millions of others – H G Wells. It seemed sacrilege to break into his sleep and so I waited until he became aware of my presence.

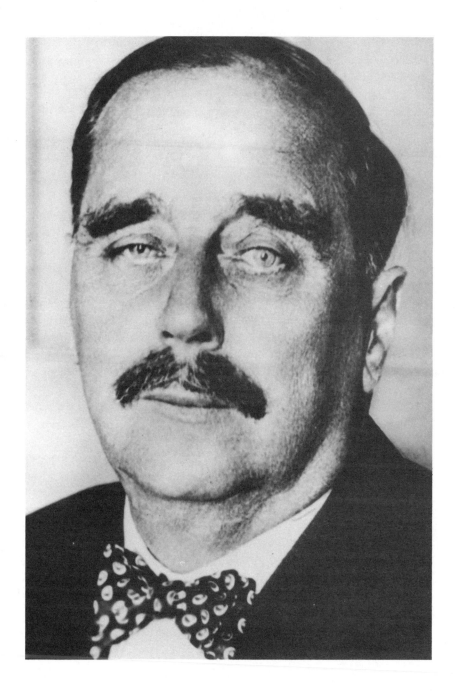

It was the gramophone which broke the impasse. It ground to a halt and the slurring of the needle brought him awake. He looked at me in some uncertainty and then said abruptly: 'Who the bloody hell are you?'

'I'm Brome – don't you remember we made a date for me to call?'

'But why interrupt me?' he said. 'Can't you see I am dying?'

He certainly was dying, with diabetes, a weak heart and but one whole lung and one kidney to live by. When his friends fell ill now, it became the occasion for a burst of bravado. As if these youngsters could hope to beat him at his own game – he who had been dying so long that nobody could hope to match the sustained achievements of sickness to which he had laid claim.

'Well,' he at last continued, 'what's it all about?'

'I'm writing a piece for the British Council about sustaining culture in wartime.'

'Culture! Oh my God! What does the word mean? Why not read this?' He pushed across to me a relatively slender manuscript. I glanced at the title, which I later checked: *Thesis on the Quality of Illusion in the Continuity of the Individual Life in the Higher Metazoa with Particular Reference to the Species Homo sapiens.*

'Read it,' he said, 'and put it in your piece. If they had listened to me we wouldn't be in this mess now.' Only later did I realise that *they* in this context were the members of the Royal Society, who were still refusing to grant him an FRS. He said quite bluntly: 'That'll show the bastards!'

He was a wreck of his old self, a loosely knit accumulation of skin and bones with his barrel of a forehead still dominating the face. But his reedy cockney voice continued to loose off broadsides in all directions.

He did so now: 'This farce of monarchy,' he said. 'You won't forget to put in your piece my detestation of monarchy, will you? Until we come to our senses about monarchy we won't get anywhere.'

In the middle of another more sustained diatribe he said, 'Let me show you the house.' It was a very remarkable house, reflecting so many sides of his personality.

We went first to the main bedroom. As befitted a man who had been a great lover and so careless about paternity, there was a four poster bed with a canopy and curtains. On the mantelpiece stood photographs of the women who had been deeply part of his emotional life. Among the graceless concubinage of his mistresses, given pride of place, was the photo of Catherine, his second wife.

On the first floor we entered the famous ladies' room, lined with mirrors.

In the lavatory, was a seat designed by himself at a special angle. In a separate side room the private telephone exchange by which he could call Margaret the maid, Mrs Johnston the housekeeper, or anyone prepared to respond to his imperative summonses.

Down to the garage next to have displayed with a touch of pride, artistic onslaughts by his own hand. They were crude sketches depicting the dawn of civilisation from beetlelike trilobites to man. Above them he had written: 'Have you the wits, have you the will to save yourselves?'

He continued his attacks as we moved from room to room. God was a superstitious irrelevance, parliament a democratic sham, Bernard Shaw a talented buffoon, women a necessary encumbrance to the life of man.

He knew that he was dying. 'Among the complications of my never very sound body is a fatty degeneration of the heart which ended the life of my father.'

The cheery, friendly, soul people found in Wells' novels seemed to have little resemblance to this man. Until the very moment when he escorted me out of the front door he continued to issue judgements which sounded like last judgements on princes, prime ministers, and generals. As for humanity – it was 'a parcel of sweeps'.

'I never met such a chap,' said Shaw. 'I could not survive meeting such another.'

At the end of a two hour meeting I echoed his sentiments. How could this be the same man who wrote *The History of Mr Polly*, *Kipps*, *The War of the Worlds*, *The Time Machine* and *A Short History of the World*? How could this be the man who so powerfully contributed to the birth of the modern mentality? I never had another chance to answer those riddles.

Richard Widmark

by Frank Barnard

HE WAS STANDING in front of me in the queue, waiting to rent a car from Avis. Short, very short, tanned and lined, he wore a narrow-brimmed hat with a hint of Florida golf courses about it, the kind of thing Bing Crosby used to favour, and the standard issue light-coloured raincoat, American tourists for the use of . . .

Except that this was no tourist. The queue shuffled closer to the counter. He waited his turn patiently. The faded blue eyes took in the rental rates and details of the Ford Escort 1.3L. He seemed . . . interested. This can't be, I thought.

I knew this man though I'd never queued with him before. I'd watched him from cheesy stalls in countless fleapits through the 40s and the 50s; snake-laughed psychopath in *Kiss of Death*, leathery US Marine 'blasting the nips' in *Halls of Montezuma*, proficient and credible gunslinger in countless Westerns, gritty cop in Don Siegel's *Madigan*. And here he stood waiting for an Avis Escort.

His wait was nearly over. The Avis doll – were they hand-picked for this Mayfair flagship? – pressed her inner switch and the Avis smile came on, just like in training, trying hard to show she was trying harder.

I couldn't catch the way it started. Heard all she said but nothing of him, apart from a murmur and mutter. At one point his hand went to his pocket, but he didn't floor her with a single blap from a .45 Colt automatic. He just fished out a biro.

So she shuffled her forms and said brightly, in a trying-harder kind of way, 'Name?' And he said, 'Widmark.' And she said, without a glimmer of reaction, 'W-I-D . . . ?' And he spelled it out for her and she wrote it down and then said, 'Christian name?' And he said, 'Richard,' and she repeated 'Richard,' and wrote that down on the form too, her tongue in the corner of her mouth.

And no-one else in that branch of Avis in North Row knew, showed any sign of knowing, that this small and patient man, biro in hand, was Widmark movie actor, sniggering killer, occasional hero, cowboy, cop. Big screen, big name, famed, a legend . . .

Except me – I knew. And then as the blonde curls bounced over the Avis forms, the washed blue gaze checked out the scene as though for hoods and trouble. Behind him the Avis doll said, 'Your vehicle will be with you momentarily, Mr uh . . . '

'Widmark,' he said again, and with that grinned at me because he knew I knew. Grinned that cheek-drawn, toothy, vulpine grin that took me back to the fag-fogged shillings in the Ritz. The grin he grinned from under snap-brimmed fedoras, GI helmets, Stetsons black and white . . .

Then he moved outside, by the garage doors where the cars arrived, and climbed aboard his shiny, trying-harder bright red Escort and motored mildly away.

Later I worked out what film he'd been making on that trip and it was rotten. He was good though, tough, convincing, Richard Widmark movie ikon, not Mr uh Widmark in the queue. But older, worn and older and it showed.

Now when I see him on the box it summons up for me glimmers of '82, waiting in the Avis queue. Most recently I saw a Western, *Last Wagon* from 1957. 'You lived in it . . . you fought in it . . . you loved in it . . . and sometimes you died in it,' cried the blurb on first release. In real life, as only I can testify, the wagon was an Escort 1.3L.

Winnie the Pooh

by Phoebe Winch

IN 1940, WHEN I was nine, I was 'evacuated' out of London, though my parents didn't use that word, implying as it did a scared East End child with a label attached like a parcel, allocated to a resentful but dutiful volunteer in the country. I was sent, without a label, to stay with friends of theirs in a village near Seaford on the south coast. This was to escape the blitz, although that part of Sussex was in the direct path of German planes unloading their unused bombs on their way back across the Channel.

The house belonged to W A Darlington – the long-serving theatre critic of the *Daily Telegraph*. The Darlingtons had a daughter, exactly my age, and also called Phoebe. For nine months we shared our lives and, rather surprisingly, a governess.

The Darlingtons also had an older daughter, Anne, who stayed in London because she was in the ATS and sometimes came down for the weekend in her glamorous uniform. (How I wanted to be a Brownie!)

The Darlingtons were close friends with the Milne family, and I knew that *Now We Are Six* was dedicated to Anne because 'now she is seven and because she is so speshal'. (Alright, sickening now, but charming then.)

One day Phoebe and I were taken to visit Anne in her flat in London. We were helping to wash-up the tea things, and just by chance I looked under her kitchen sink. There, in an enamelled washing-up bowl, were Pooh, Piglet, Kanga and Roo. I don't remember seeing Eeyore, but perhaps he was there. Tigger certainly wasn't.

These weren't any old toys tucked away out of sight. They were instantly recognisable. E H Shepard had drawn them from life, as it were. Anne explained, in a very matter-of-fact way that she was looking after them while Christopher was away fighting the war. They lived under the sink because it made a good air-raid shelter for them.

I was allowed to pick them up, but was too surprised to actually play with them.

They seemed to be taken for granted – no-one had mentioned that Pooh and Piglet would be in Anne's flat. I had just found them, and it seemed bad manners to make too much of a fuss about them.

Also, they were rather battered and balding, well-used, and had obviously belonged to another child and been much loved. But, like every other Winnie the Pooh reader, I, too, had played with them, loved them, and shared their adventures in the Forest. I even knew how they thought, and what they talked about.

It was all rather disturbing – like bumping into Jo March of *Little Women* (my favourite book at that time) in Harrods, or meeting Huckleberry Finn in Hyde Park. I heard much later that Pooh, Piglet and Kanga survived the war, and used to tour America in a glass case. I wonder where they are now.

Donald Wolfit

by Robin Rook

I T WAS MORE than 50 years ago. The little old lady in tweed suit and felt hat who accompanied me to the matinée was my go-between. She had been a childhood friend of Don's from Newark days but how I came to know her and who precisely she was is a mystery. We went to see *Macbeth* or *Hamlet* or *Volpone*, I forget which, and had been graciously invited backstage.

We penetrated the dingy interior and mounted the stairs to the principal dressing-room. The door was not particularly memorable but the response to my friend's timid knock most certainly was: 'Enter!' He was seated on a very ordinary chair, surrounded by the costumes of his trade, but his relaxed pose and august presence filled the room. The chair became a throne. Our host ceased to be an actor and became a personification of the Prince Regent. I was not visiting, I was being presented.

After a polite exchange of greetings, he looked me up and down and said words to the effect: 'So this young man wants to go on to the stage. It is a great profession but unless you are called, you're wasting your time. And something must be done about that voice of yours,' – I had just returned to Oxford after four years' service as an officer – 'it reeks of privilege. What are you going to do when you carry a spear or pretend to be a ruffian? I can't imagine you saying: "Faith, sir, we were carousing till the second cock: and drink, sir, is a great provoker of three things." Say it.' I tried. 'No, no, that will never do. A mouse could do better.' I felt like one. 'Let me hear you breathe. Breathe! Enough. Here, put your hand here.' He pointed to a spot frighteningly close to his belly.

I was intimidated, so intimidated that I did as I was told. He inhaled a massive amount of air and the flesh concealed beneath his dressing-gown expanded to an alarming extent. I thought he was about to rise from the chair like a hot-air balloon, but slowly it began to subside as a low, melodic note issued from his mouth. It seemed to last an eternity.

Shortly after the demonstration, we were dismissed, not summarily but kindly. He had enjoyed impressing a young and naive aspirant to the profession. But it is his presence that I remember most vividly. Imagine someone who can dominate a great Victorian theatre with a whisper, who can demand applause by hanging onto the curtain like a silent opera singer, and then stuff such a man into a small dressing-room; be not surprised then that, as I descended the stairs, these words came to me, 'I could be bound in a nutshell, and count myself a king of infinite space . . .' Perhaps we had been to *Hamlet*, not to *Macbeth*. Who knows?